# *The* LOST TOWN
## Bringing Back Trochenbrod

Also by Avrom Bendavid-Val

*The Heavens Are Empty,* 2010

Books in the fields of environmental management
and regional development include:

*Achieving Environmental Excellence,* 2003

*Green Profits,* 2001

*More With Less,* 1987

*Regional and Local Economic Analysis for Practitioners,* 1991

*Rural Area Development Planning,* 1991

# The LOST TOWN
## Bringing Back Trochenbrod

AVROM BENDAVID-VAL

Bacon Press Books
Washington, DC
2015

Copyright © 2015 Avrom Bendavid-Val

All rights reserved. No part of this publication may be reproduced, stored in a retrieval system, or transmitted by any means—electronic, mechanical, photographic (photocopying), recording, or otherwise—without prior permission in writing from the author.

The words of individuals, excerpts of written documents, and photographs appear with the written permission of the individuals quoted, the creators of the documents or photographs, their next of kin, or authorized descendants.

The views and observations expressed by individuals interviewed, or whose recollections were recorded by someone else and provided to the author, must be understood as reflecting solely their own perceptions and memories.

Published in the United States by Bacon Press Books, Washington, DC
www.baconpressbooks.com

Editor: Lorraine Fico-White, www.magnificomanuscripts.com
Cover Design and Maps: Alan Pranke, www.amp13.com
Cover Photo: Ruchel Abrams
Author Photo: Leah Bendavid-Val
Book Design and Layout: Lorie DeWorken, www.mindthemargins.com

ISBN: 978-0-9863060-4-4

Library of Congress Control Number: 2015946035

PRINTED IN THE UNITED STATES OF AMERICA

# Table of Contents

Dedication . . . . . . . . . . . . . . . . . . . . . . . vii

Introduction — *My Search Begins* . . . . . . . . . . . . . . . . . 1

Chapter 1 — *Trochenbrod Takes Shape* . . . . . . . . . . . . 7

Chapter 2 — *Into the Twentieth Century* . . . . . . . . . 30

Chapter 3 — *Booming Between the Wars* . . . . . . . . . 49

Chapter 4 — *Dusk and Darkness* . . . . . . . . . . . . . . 76

Chapter 5 — *Darkness: Khaim Fights* . . . . . . . . . . 100

Chapter 6 — *Darkness: Basia-Ruchel Survives* . . . . . . 110

Chapter 7 — *Darkness: Ryszard Witnesses* . . . . . . . . 122

Chapter 8 — *The Story Continues* . . . . . . . . . . . . 130

Trochenbrod Chronology . . . . . . . . . . . . . . . . 137

Sources . . . . . . . . . . . . . . . . . . . . . . . . . . . 141

Acknowledgments . . . . . . . . . . . . . . . . . . . . 145

About the Author . . . . . . . . . . . . . . . . . . . . 149

# DEDICATION

This book is dedicated to my father, YomTov (Yonteleh) Beider.
He went from Trochenbrod to Palestine in 1932,
and then immigrated to the United States in 1939.
He died 30 years later in Washington, DC.

# INTRODUCTION
# MY SEARCH BEGINS

As I was growing up, my father did not often mention the town Trochenbrod (pronounced **Traw**khenbrawd) in Eastern Poland where he was born and raised. But when he did, his longing and affection for it were unmistakable. After my father passed away, I realized I knew nothing about his beloved hometown. He had never volunteered information about it, and I had never asked. Although none of my relatives knew where Trochenbrod had been located, other than "in Poland someplace," they were certain nothing was there anymore. I was told that after the Nazis murdered all Trochenbrod's Jews, they destroyed all its buildings, and the memory of it was lost.

How could that be? I wondered. How could all traces of a town and its people vanish? If the town was destroyed in the Holocaust, wouldn't something—derelict buildings, house foundations, low stone walls—still be found there? And what happened to Christian neighbors of the Jews who lived in Trochenbrod? They weren't destroyed by the Nazis; maybe their descendants were still there and could tell me something about Trochenbrod in the days when Jews also lived there. I had to find out. I had to see for myself.

And I did. First I researched in the Library of Congress, the National Archives, and the Mormon Family Research Center. I found Trochenbrod on old maps and discovered that it was also known as Sofiyovka. I found its coordinates and discovered it was no longer in Poland but in the northwest corner of Ukraine, about 20 miles from the city of Lutsk—today, a city of 300,000. I figured out the combination of planes, trains, and automobiles I would need to get to Trochenbrod, which seemed to be far from any paved road. I convinced my brother to join me.

After a year of planning, arranging, and preparing, we found ourselves there, in that northwest corner of Ukraine, trudging through the high wild grass of a broad meadow deep in the forest. We were accompanied by an elderly peasant woman from a nearby village who had agreed to show us the way. When I finally looked down the scraggly trail that was once the long, straight street in Trochenbrod, I was overcome with emotion. I couldn't move or speak for several minutes, and then felt the trickle of a tear on each cheek. Imagine, there had been a town in this empty and abandoned place, the town where my father was born and raised!

*The* LOST TOWN

AERIAL PHOTO OF TROCHENBROD AS IT APPEARS TODAY.
*Photograph by the author.*

I wanted to know everything about it. What did Trochenbrod look like? How many people had lived there, and how did they earn their livings? Who besides Jews had lived there? What sorts of relations did Trochenbrod have with other villages? How did the town begin, and how did the enormous tragedy happen that made Trochenbrod vanish? How could I find out everything there was to know about this lost town?

I didn't know then that over the next 15 years, I would travel all over America and to other countries finding answers to my questions—questions I hadn't thought to ask my father. I collected photographs, memoirs, recordings, and videos from people whose parents or grandparents or great-grandparents had immigrated to America from Trochenbrod. Again and again I visited the clearing in the forest where Trochenbrod had stood, looking for signs of the life that had disappeared. I visited the surrounding villages, where I talked to elderly Ukrainians and Poles who remembered visiting Trochenbrod as children. I interviewed the few people still alive who were born in Trochenbrod and now lived in America, Brazil, Israel, Poland, and Ukraine. Every time I discovered something new, Trochenbrod became more real to me. Little by little the town where my father grew up rose from the mist of lost history: I discovered that Trochenbrod was like no other place on earth, and almost no one knew about it.

When my father left Trochenbrod in the early 1930s, it was the largest and busiest town in the farming region that surrounded it. Dozens of businesses and government services lined its street, including a post office, a police station, and a public school. People came from villages all around to bring their children to school, to buy and sell goods, to collect their mail, to send telegrams, and to order custom-made products like clothes and furniture. There were farm fields behind the homes in Trochenbrod, still there from its early years as a farming village; but Trochenbrod had grown into a bustling town, the "big city" for children who lived in the villages around it.

Trochenbrod was different from all other towns in Europe because everyone who lived there was Jewish. And because it

*The* LOST TOWN

was hidden deep in the forest, this town of 5,000 people was almost unknown beyond the nearby Ukrainian and Polish villages. Government authorities paid little attention to Trochenbrod, and Jewish customs were the only ones that mattered. All of Trochenbrod observed Jewish holidays and celebrated Jewish festivals like one huge family. Children played in the yards and fields, chuckling, yelling in Yiddish, and running up and down Trochenbrod's one long street in complete safety and freedom. At dinner time, the aroma of Jewish cooking filled every corner of the little town and wafted into the surrounding forest.

By the end of World War II, everything was gone. Everything—Trochenbrod's houses, synagogues, shops, and public buildings, as well as its people—had been destroyed. All that remained was a double row of trees and bushes surrounded by a clearing where its farm fields had been.

Once I had pieced together Trochenbrod's story, I knew I had to share it. I would rescue the memory of Trochenbrod, and in a way, bring Trochenbrod back to life. *The Lost Town* is the story of 130 years of highs and lows and finally the destruction of Trochenbrod and its people. It is about the will people have and the struggles they will endure to be free to live their lives as they believe they should.

Earlier, I wrote a book for adults about Trochenbrod both to rescue the memory of the town for its own sake and because it is part of the historical experience we all share.

AVROM BENDAVID-VAL

To the younger readers of this new book: I hope you will realize that the story of your parents and grandparents and where they came from plays a role in defining who you are, even if you are unaware of it. I hope you will begin now—and not make the mistake of waiting as long as I did—to learn about this story—your own story.

CHAPTER ONE
# Trochenbrod Takes Shape

## The Beginning

I knew from comments my father had made that there were other people who, like him, had grown up in Trochenbrod and went to Palestine in the 1920s or 1930s as pioneers, with the idea of rebuilding the Jewish homeland there. When I started my search, one of the first things I did was to fly to Israel and interview older people who were born in Trochenbrod and left before World War II. They were all members of an organization started in Palestine in the 1930s. Back then, they would meet regularly to stay in touch, share news about Trochenbrod, and help newcomers to settle in. My father was one of the newcomers they had helped. When the State of Israel was created, they became a formal organization under Israeli law. They built a meeting hall near Tel Aviv and took the name Bet Tal.[1]

---

1. In Hebrew, Bet Tal is written as House of TL. TL is an acronym for "Trochenbrod and Lozisht." Lozisht was a smaller sister village connected to Trochenbrod.

When I arrived to interview people, Bet Tal had hundreds of members, but by this time most of the members were children or grandchildren or even great-grandchildren of the original Trochenbrod pioneers. Only a small number of the original pioneers remained, people who remembered what life was like in Trochenbrod; they could tell me about growing up there and what they had learned from their parents and neighbors about the town's early history. The Bet Tal organization gave me a list of their older members, and I interviewed every one of them. I was surprised to learn that Trochenbrod started as a tiny farming village at a time when the farming villages around it had already existed for hundreds of years.

TROCHENBROD LOCATED ON A MAP OF EUROPE.
*Map by Alan Pranke.*

*The* LOST TOWN

———

In 1804, Czar Alexander I issued a decree forcing rural Jews in Russia to move from the villages and small towns where they lived to shtetls[2] in the larger towns and big cities. There government officials could watch and control them better, and tax them heavily. Jews arrived in these shtetls with little money and little chance of earning more. They could not earn their livings from work they had done in the rural towns and villages they came from, work like constucting houses and farm buildings, operating flour mills, and trading produce at regional markets.

But the Czar was also anxious to increase farm production in Russia. So he allowed Jewish families that would take up farming on unused land to be exempt from the harsh new rules. Farming was unfamiliar to Jews. For nearly 2,000 years, they had not been farmers. In Russia and in many other countries, Jews had not even been allowed to own land. And any unused land had been abandoned because the soil was bad or it was far away from markets. Despite all this, some Jews were determined to escape the Czar's decree and stay as far away from the Czar's government as possible. They saw rural areas and farming as their best opportunity for that.

In 1810, a few Jewish men from the cities of Lutsk, Rovno, and Kolki quietly trekked to an isolated spot inside the triangle formed

---

2. A shtetl is a Jewish neighborhood—a small Jewish village—within a larger town or city.

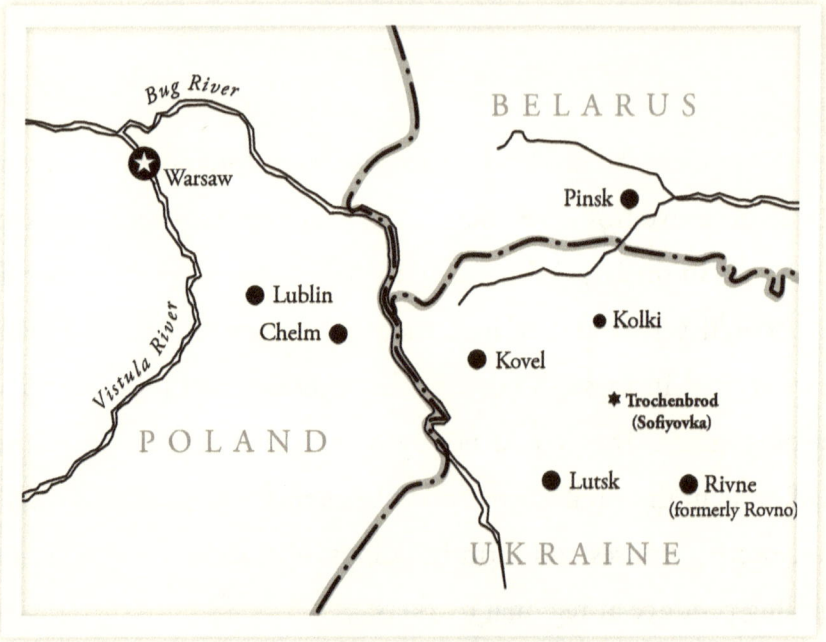

THE REGION AROUND TROCHENBROD.
*Map by Alan Pranke.*

by those cities and began homesteading. They settled in a marshy clearing surrounded by dense pine forests. Trees could not grow in the low wet soil of the clearing, and neither could crops unless the soil was drained. A trip to any market fair would be long, difficult, and dangerous. The land was the property of a local landholder named Trofim, who was happy to let the Jewish settlers, for a small fee, try to farm on his useless land. A creek tumbled out of the forest and ran through the clearing and then disappeared into the woods again. There was a shallow spot where travelers on a trail connecting villages in the area could ford the creek. The place was known as Trofim Ford. The word for ford in Russian is *brod*. Over time the Yiddish-speaking settlers transformed the name Trofim Brod into Trochenbrod.

As it turned out, Czar Alexander's 1804 decree was the first of a long series of decrees, some contradicting ones that had been issued before, from a succession of czars stretching over the next 100 years. The decrees influenced how Trochenbrod developed, and encouraged new waves of settlers to the town.

## EARLY YEARS

The first baby was born in Trochenbrod in 1813. Trochenbrod's stories were passed down from one generation to the next, until eventually, near the end of the 1800s, they were recorded in a large book. Town clerks, one after the other, continued to record major developments and events in Trochenbrod. The book was stored in one of Trochenbrod's main synagogues. Unfortunately, the synagogue was destroyed with everything in it by a fire around 1915. Perhaps the synagogue was a casualty of one of the artillery shells that hit Trochenbrod during World War I. Many Trochenbroders were familiar with the stories in the book—stories of Trochenbrod's history—and told these stories to their children. Some of those children grew up to be Jewish pioneers in Palestine and were still there and happy to tell me what they knew when I visited.

In the months before I went to Israel, I had already collected several memoirs written by Trochenbroders who had immigrated to America. The memoirs often included stories about Trochenbrod's early history. I started each interview in Israel by reading one or two excerpts from the memoirs. I asked each Trochenbroder I interviewed how the excerpt I had just read compared with Trochenbrod's history as he or she knew it. Out of this grew a well-defined description of Trochenbrod's early years, a description reinforced by other memoirs that eventually came my way.

It was hard for the first settlers. Imagine the fathers and sons who went to the marshy clearing to prepare the place so they could bring their families. They drove their horse-drawn wagons to Trofim Ford wearing their city clothes, unloaded their tools and belongings, gathered wood, lit a fire, and slept under the stars the first night. Wolves and other wild animals roamed the area, and snakes were everywhere. Those first Jewish settlers must have been terrified by the howls, grunts, and slithering noises they heard all night long.

But they were probably also filled with happiness that maybe, just maybe, in this place they would be able to escape the day-to-day cruelties of the Czar's government officials. The next day, after morning prayers and something to eat, they must have taken a good look around and wondered, Can we really do this?

Although these city Jews knew almost nothing about farming, they pushed on. They cleared brush and cut trees from the forest to make primitive shelters for themselves, and later they built simple houses with dirt floors for their families. Ukrainian and Polish villagers who passed by on the trails gave them farming tips, but these

AREA WHERE SETTLERS FIRST ARRIVED. THE BULRUSHES MARK A CREEK.
*Photograph by the author.*

Jews learned how to farm mainly through hard work and learning from their mistakes.

The number of Jews who settled at Trofim Ford grew slowly until 1827. In that year, Czar Nicholas I, who followed Alexander I, issued another anti-Semitic decree. This one required that Jewish boys be drafted into the Russian Army while they were teenagers and remain there until they were 45 years old. The Czar saw this as a practical way of eliminating his "Jewish problem." By the time the forty-five-year-old was released from the army, he would have been away from his relatives and his religion for 30 years. If he had managed to stay alive during his time in the army, he would no longer be Jewish. This decree had the same special provision as

Czar Alexander's 1804 decree: it did not apply to boys from Jewish families that settled as farmers on unused land. As a result, another wave of Jewish families came to Trochenbrod. Soon after this, new local government rules allowed the Jewish settlers to buy the land where they had established their village.

So Trochenbrod grew, with ever more houses lining up along both sides of the village's one street that became a bit longer each year. The forest surrounded Trochenbrod, and each family's farm fields stretched back behind their house to the edge of the forest. Even the city Jews who settled Trochenbrod knew they could not farm on marshy land. They dug long canals that ran along the sides of their farm fields and drained the water into the forest. This backbreaking work gave Trochenbrod families drier fields for their crops. The Jewish settler families did not know their canals would offer a pathway to life for their descendants during the Holocaust more than 100 years in the future.

As time passed, these Trochenbrod city settlers gradually learned how to farm, and even became known in the surrounding villages for their good farming skills. However, the soil was poor and the settlers found it impossible to survive only from their crops. To give themselves more of a livelihood, Trochenbroders turned to the work they had done in the cities. Some set up small shops and others offered skilled trades, like carpentry and making windows, to Ukrainian and Polish villages in the region. Still others raised animals, especially cattle, to supplement their income. Fodder was

HEAD OF A SHORT-HANDLED HOE FOUND IN A TROCHENBROD FIELD, 2009.
*Photograph by the author.*

easy to grow even in poor soil, and it did not need to be taken to market since it was consumed by their livestock. From raising cattle for meat, they gradually developed businesses in dairy products like milk and butter, and also leather and leather products like belts and boots. Over the years, Trochenbrod became known in the region as *the* place to go to buy high-quality boots for withstanding the mud that was everywhere during many months of the year.

---

Trochenbrod would not be like the unchanged Ukrainian and Polish farming villages in the region. Though no one in Trochenbrod ever made a conscious decision about it, early Trochenbroders set their village on a different path, one that enabled them to improve their lives. The farming village of Trochenbrod developed into a town with shop owners, traders, and craftsmen who were also farmers. All the while, Trochenbroders continued to observe Jewish law and customs strictly, just as they had done in the cities they came from.

In 1835, 8 years after he issued his decree requiring Jewish boys to serve 30 years in his army, Czar Nicholas I issued a new "Law of the Jews." Among many other things, this decree required all rural Jews to live in official settlements and apply for government permits when they wanted to travel. The Czar's idea this time was to make it impossible for Jews to establish themselves as farmers to avoid the anti-Semitic laws and then secretly move back to the cities. The travel permits would enable the government to track them. But Trochenbrod had become a proud and strongly independent village that ran its own affairs. Its people hated the idea that they would need permission to travel from their village to the cities in the area, where they had relatives and business connections. But there was nothing they could do. To make matters worse, Trochenbrod was forced to come out of hiding—it had to become an official Russian agricultural settlement, a farming "colony," recognized by the government.

Early in my Trochenbrod research, I went to the Library of Congress in Washington, DC, to look for old maps of Poland and Russia that might show where Trochenbrod had been located once it had become an official settlement. Sitting around the corner of the large table, I noticed a woman who studied a map I had looked at earlier and set aside. First I thought nothing of it. But then, I saw a broad smile come over her face when she looked at it—it was an old Russian map covering the Horyn River, which ran about 30 miles east of the place where Trochenbrod stood.

I couldn't help myself. "Did you find what you're looking for?" I asked her.

"Yes I did," she answered with a pleasant smile, as if we were old friends continuing a conversation. "I'm trying to figure out the exact location of an old village, one that was abandoned about 175 years ago. I know approximately where it was located, but it was so small that it probably was not shown on a map, especially a map made by the Russian government. I keep trying, though." She told me she was having trouble finding a map created at just the right time by just the right people. Different mapmakers didn't always include the same details.

"On this map," she pointed to the one on the table in front of her, "I can see where the village I'm interested in was possibly located based on the contour lines and the surrounding villages. I can't know for sure, but it's fun at least to see exactly where the village *might* have been. What are you looking for?"

"I'm looking for a small village or town not too far from the city of Lutsk. My father was born there."

"What was the name of the village?" she asked.

"Oh, it was just a small out-of-the-way place. I'm sure you never heard of it. Everyone who lived there was Jewish. It was called Trochenbrod. What was name of the village you're looking for?"

"It was also a small out-of-the-way place. I'm looking for a Mennonite village called Sofiyovka. We Mennonites never believed in war or fighting, so in the eighteenth and early nineteenth centuries, many of our ancestors fled Germany and established small villages in Ukraine where they tried to practice the most modern form of agriculture known at that time."

"Maybe there were lots of villages named Sofiyovka in Ukraine because that was also Trochenbrod's Russian name. Do you know where your village's name came from?"

She didn't, but we decided to have a cup of coffee together and talk about our research on our two villages with the same name. We exchanged telephone numbers and said we should stay in touch.

In truth, I never expected to hear from her again, but a week later I answered the phone and heard her excited voice on the line.

"I could not get the coincidence we discovered out of my mind, so this morning I called a friend in Winnipeg who is an authority on Mennonite history. In fact, he's the author of the Mennonite Atlas. I always understood that the Mennonites from Sofiyovka had moved to a larger Mennonite community in southern Ukraine. I asked my friend if there was any more to their story. 'There sure is,' he said."

He told her that in the mid-1820s, the 21 Mennonite families living in the village of Sofiyovka, on the Horyn River, abandoned their village. They decided to move on because after working for more than 15 years, they found that no matter how hard they worked or

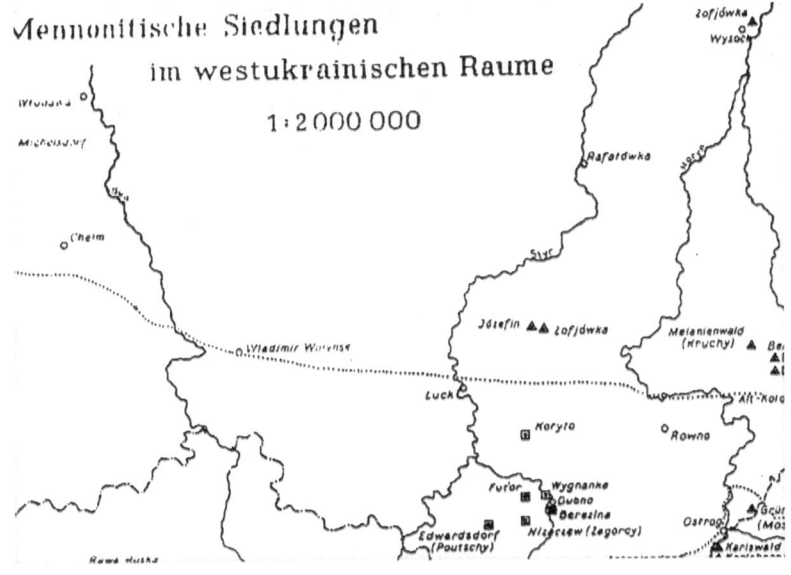

SEGMENT OF A MAP OF MENNONITE SETTLEMENTS IN THE MID-1800S SHOWS THE ORIGINAL SETTLEMENT OF SOFIYOVKA (ZOFIJÓWKA, UPPER RIGHT), AND THE TWO NEW SETTLEMENTS, YOSEFIN (JÓZEFIN) AND SOFIYOVKA, NORTHEAST OF LUTSK (LUCK).
*From the Mennonite Historical Alas, 1996.*

how cleverly they farmed, they simply could not make a living in Sofiyovka—the soil was just not good enough. They found some empty land owned by a local landholder named Trofim in a remote area about 20 miles northeast of Lutsk and established 2 small settlements there. They named one of the new settlements Yosefin, for unknown reasons. They named the other settlement Sofiyovka, in remembrance of the village those Mennonite families had left. Sofiyovka was two or three miles east from Yosefin. About 10 years later, these Mennonite families abandoned their new villages because again the soil turned out to be too poor to support their farms. Then they trekked to southern

Ukraine in order to join relatives in a larger Mennonite settlement, and from there they eventually immigrated to America.

This was exciting news! I found the village of Yosefin on one of the old maps I had copied at the Library of Congress. Years later, I learned that the village had been resettled by other people after the Mennonites left and survived as a farming village until World War II.

The Mennonite village of Sofiyovka, just east of Yosefin, seemed to have been located very close to Trochenbrod. If the Mennonite settlers left after about 10 years, that would have been at about the same time that Trochenbrod's elders and the Russian government agreed that Trochenbrod would become an official colony. Now it would appear on maps. Official colonies that appeared on Russian maps had to have Russian names. In all likelihood, Trochenbrod was given, or took, the name of the Mennonite settlement located very near to it and probably took over its abandoned land. From then on everyone, both Jews and neighboring gentiles, knew the village, and later the town, as both Trochenbrod and Sofiyovka.

―――

When I was in the Trochenbrod area recently, I became curious to see what local people knew of their history when Jews lived there before World War II and the Holocaust. I saw a villager passing by on a horse-drawn farm wagon. Little pieces of hay clung to his work shirt, which was open at the neck with sleeves rolled up over muscular arms. His arms and weathered face were deeply sun-tanned.

His torn khaki pants were rolled up a few inches and clearly had seen a lot of work on the farm. With the help of my Ukrainian friend, I asked if he knew where Trochenbrod was. He tilted his head sideways and looked up at the sky, as if he hoped to see the answer to my question written there. He stroked his chin and murmured "Trochenbrod" a few times, trying hard to remember where he had heard that name before. His wife, who was sitting comfortably in a faded flower-patterned work dress on a pile of hay in the wagon behind the driver's bench, gently whipped her husband with a stalk of grass—she seemed to be trying to prod his memory.

She muttered a hint to him. "The Jews, Sofiyovka."

"Ah, yes, the Jews, Sofiyovka, Trochenbrod!" he shouted in triumph. "Down that way." He pointed beyond some decaying barns and chicken coops of an abandoned collective farm left behind from when the Soviet Union had ruled there. I'll never forget it. He pointed over the old collective-farm buildings as if he meant to say, "Down that way. To find Trochenbrod, you have to skip over the period when we were ruled by the Soviet Union and go back to before World War II, when we were ruled by Poland."

---

Trochenbrod/Sofiyovka became an official colony in 1835. The earliest census records I could find were from much later in the nineteenth century, but a reasonable guess is that in 1835, 30 to 50 families, about 250 people, lived in Trochenbrod. That was roughly the number of people in many nearby villages. In the case of Trochenbrod, however, as in no other village, everyone was Jewish. In fact, by the time Trochenbrod became an official colony, it had already grown so much since its first days that another small Jewish hamlet had been started close by, a sort of suburb of Trochenbrod. It was started by children of early Trochenbrod settlers who needed their own land to farm. It became officially a colony the same time as Trochenbrod and was called Lozisht by the Jews, Ignatovka by others. The settlers in Trochenbrod and Lozisht were very close; many were relatives. People thought of the two as one larger settlement, Trochenbrod-Lozisht, and many descendants of Trochenbrod and Lozisht still think of them that way today.

## Mid-Century

In the mid-1800s, the houses in Trochenbrod looked like the houses in other Ukrainian villages. Their front yards, though, were smaller than in other villages: Trochenbroders wanted to be able to see from their houses what was going on in the town's one street and call out to the children, peddlers, friends, and relatives they saw there. Behind each house were long, narrow farm fields. The drainage canals ran alongside the farm fields to the forest half-a-mile or more away. Most Trochenbrod families built small sheds—out-houses, tool sheds, and storage sheds immediately behind their houses.

Trochenbrod's street was nothing more than a broad muddy path. Trochenbroders dug deep drainage ditches along the sides of

*The* LOST TOWN

SKETCH OF TROCHENBROD IN THE 19TH CENTURY.
*Adapted from* Hailan V'shoreshav *(The Tree and Its Roots), published by Bet Tal, Israel, 1988.*

the street in front of the houses to help drain away the water after a rain to make the street passable as quickly as possible. Because Trochenbrod was in a low area that was originally marshy, rainwater tended to settle in big puddles that stayed a long time. Each Trochenbrod family put boards over the ditch to make a small bridge to their house. The early settlers soon began to plant willow trees along the street to help protect against erosion but also to add life, color, and shade in the summer. For the generations of Trochenbroders that followed, and for the sons and daughters of the town who later immigrated to America, Israel, and other countries, those trees lining the street were an important part of their memory of Trochenbrod. Today it is descendants of those trees that tell us where Trochenbrod stood.

The early Jews of Trochenbrod were Hassidic Jews. They believed that spirituality and joy, in addition to Torah study, were key elements of Judaism. Hassidic men often wore long dark jackets, white shirts, and large round fur hats, as many Hassids in both America and Israel do today. The appearance of Hassidic dress was annoying to the Czar and his officials, and they thought banning such clothes would help suppress Jewish practice. In an 1850 decree, the Czar outlawed Hassidic dress. The decree was resisted in Trochenbrod as it was elsewhere, but still it had an impact. Hassidic dress and practices diminished in Trochenbrod over the following decades, yet Trochenbroders remained religiously observant. Even 90 years later, when some young people, especially young men, were no longer observant, everyone went to synagogue on the Sabbath and took part in all the religious holidays. It was required by the heads of Trochenbrod households: no family would be shamed by having a son out and about when the men in the town were at prayer in the synagogues.

As America's Civil War was ending in 1865, Czar Alexander II issued yet another edict for the Jews under his rule. This one allowed Jews who owned farmland, like Trochenbrod's Jews, to change their status from "farm villager" to "town dweller" without giving up their land. This time, the Czar's idea was to allow Jews who had become farmers to keep their farms and still live in towns and cities; from there, they could travel freely without special permits. But there was a price. In the towns and cities, Jewish boys who were not first-born sons would be subject to conscription laws and could be easily rounded up and drafted into the Russian Army. It was to avoid this that many Jewish families had moved to Trochenbrod and taken up farming in the first place.

Trochenbrod's elders tried to convince the Czar's government to change the status of Sofiyovka from a colony to a town, so their people could continue to live there and would not need the reviled special permit to travel. By this time, Trochenbroders needed to travel often to cities in the area to sell their dairy products. Trochenbrod's elders appealed to the government and were granted official status as a town. They figured they'd find other ways to avoid conscription. Typical methods were to not record the births of boys; to hide their sons or have them flee the town when government agents came looking for conscripts; to send their sons to far away cities for long periods of religious study in yeshivas; and to regularly change family names, so that every son born would be recorded as "firstborn."

## END OF THE 1800s

At the end of the 1800s, Trochenbrod was a bustling commercial center, more dependent on commerce and crafts than on agriculture for its economic well-being. Dairy and leather products were the largest part of its economy. Of the several leather tanneries in Trochenbrod, the largest was owned by the Shwartz family, who employed seven people making high quality leather. Young David

RUSSIAN MAP SHOWS SOFIYOVKA'S ONE LONG, STRAIGHT STREET
(LOWER RIGHT), 1890.
*Found by the author in the Library of Congress, Washington, DC.*

Shwartz had heard stories that filtered back from Jewish immigrants. Jewish immigrants had been streaming to America since 1880 to escape the government-approved attacks on Russian Jews called pogroms and to find greater freedom and economic prospects. From these stories, David understood America was the land of opportunity. In 1907, at age 27, he left Trochenbrod for Columbus, Ohio, where several other immigrant families from Trochenbrod lived.

David became prosperous in America. In 1934, he visited Palestine to see the new Jewish settlements and cities there. On the way, David and his wife spent a few weeks visiting his old friends and neighbors in Trochenbrod. This was long after World War I had ended, but no one foresaw that in only five years Germany would invade Poland and set off World War II. A few years after his visit to Trochenbrod, David wrote the first draft of a memoir in which he combined memories of his 1934 visit to Trochenbrod with memories of the Trochenbrod of his youth before World War I. He put the manuscript in a drawer, meaning to reread and put finishing touches on it soon. But for some reason it was not until 15 years later that David Shwartz finally took the manuscript from the drawer and finished his memoir. While David's manuscript waited in its drawer, Trochenbrod disappeared in the Holocaust, and the State of Israel was born.

Years later, one of David's grandchildren heard about my Trochenbrod research and sent me a copy of the memoir. In the following excerpt from that memoir, first drafted in 1939, David recalls some of Trochenbrod's people as he knew them growing up. His memories of Trochenbrod characters tell some of the story of how Trochenbroders earned their livings in the late 1800s and early 1900s. It fascinated me immediately because while almost everyone in Trochenbrod still worked small farms, other occupations had become so important that farming was not mentioned once in the following excerpt:

> There was long-bearded Motty, in summer a house-painter and in winter, he worked in my father's tannery; Shmuel Shimon, the shoemaker, a very good man, who used to go from house to house to wake people up for prayers; Yosel, the teacher; Abe, who owned

an oil press; Itzik, the weaver; Shmerl, the *Shokhet*[3]; Wolf, another shoemaker; Khaimke, the bathhouse keeper; Moshe Motia, the tailor; "long" Khuna, the butcher; Khaim Yoel, the carpenter; Wolf, the scribe; Ziviz, the midwife; Motke Zirelis, the candlemaker; Berel from the feed-mill; Shmuel, the healer; Benzion, who had a tannery; Shmilike, who owned a tannery, a little synagogue, and a bathhouse; Yaakov Leib, the cooper; Hirschke Katzke, who kept a bar; Yankel, the blacksmith; and Itzy, with the nose.

According to census data I found, by the end of the century the combined Trochenbrod and Lozisht population was about 1,600 Jews. I'm still amazed when I remember that this small but full-fledged town of 1,600 people had flowered in a few generations from a handful of Jews who knew nothing about farming but decided to settle in a marshy clearing in the forest to escape a czar's edict.

---

3. A Shokhet is a slaughterer for kosher meat.

THE WEINER FAMILY, TROCHENBROD, LATE 1800S.
*Photograph provided by Miriam Weiner Bernhardt, their granddaughter.*

## CHAPTER TWO
# INTO THE TWENTIETH CENTURY

### BEFORE WORLD WAR I

Trochenbrod's population now grew steadily because it enjoyed a relative economic boom. In the early twentieth century, it boasted more and bigger flour mills, feed mills, and oil presses than before; cattle traders who traveled long distances to buy and sell livestock; a large leather-making and leather-goods industry, including shoe, boot, and bridle makers; and three dairies that sold eggs, milk, and butter to the surrounding villages and cities. Trochenbrod even had two glass factories that took wood for fuel from the nearby forest and used the sandy soil near Trochenbrod for glass-making. Among the many shops were glaziers, wood dealers, butchers, fabrics, medicines, and hardware—almost anything a villager would need. In fact, villagers came from all around the region to shop in Trochenbrod. Trochenbroders went to all the different outdoor markets in different towns on different days of the week to sell their goods and buy other goods to sell in Trochenbrod. In addition to eggs and dairy products, Trochenbroders now traded a wide variety of goods with the surrounding cities. For example, they sold tanned hides to leather workshops in Lutsk and horsehair to brush-making workshops in Rovno.

REMNANT FROM THE SITE OF TROCHENBROD'S GLASS FACTORY.
*Recovered and photographed by the author.*

Trochenbrod now had more regular contact with the outside world than before—Jewish newspapers from Warsaw reached Trochenbrod, carrying news of both the Jewish world and the larger world, and Trochenbroders became more aware of the major military, diplomatic, and political happenings outside. Some Trochenbrod boys and young men studied at yeshivas in cities like Lublin, Poland, and Vilna (Vilnius), Lithuania. A number of

Trochenbroders immigrated to the West, especially to America, in this period, and they sent letters home to Trochenbrod describing life and events in their new countries.

Despite its relative isolation, as the new century began, Trochenbrod entered the modern world step-by-step. Yet this unique little town retained the essential Jewish qualities its founders began with. All the townspeople celebrated weddings and Jewish holidays together, becoming a rabbi and scholar was the highest aspiration for many young men, and most young men were sent to yeshivas to study Torah. When a famous rabbi visited from a big city, the whole town went out to greet him. Trochenbrod families competed to have the visiting rabbi as a guest in their house, and the town celebrated his visit night after night during his stay. All the memoirs I gathered told this same story, and the authors all commented wistfully on what Sabbath was like in Trochenbrod.

On the Sabbath, Trochenbrod's Jews did no work, lit no fires, shouldered no burdens. Though the modern world stubbornly seeped into the hidden little town, still, in all of Trochenbrod Saturday, the Sabbath, remained a day only for peace, rest, family, and prayer. In Trochenbrod, everyone lived for the Sabbath. Here is what David Shwartz wrote in his nostalgic memoir about Sabbath in Trochenbrod early in the twentieth century:

> Each family possessed a wooden mortar, made from the stump of a tree, and they made a pestle for crushing in this. Barley was put into the hot oven after the bread was taken out. Inside the oven,

the barley dried and after that it was crushed in the mortar with the pestle. This work was always kept for Thursday so that they would have enough crushed barley for the Sabbath meal.

On Friday everyone finished work early, and after lunch everyone, young and old, would dash to the bathhouse. After the bath, they then got dressed in Sabbath array and went to the synagogue. In summer it was a pleasure to hear the friendly greetings "Shalom aleichem" and the music of the voices of the fathers and children was carried from the synagogues the length of the street and would enter into every limb.

After supper we sat out on our front steps and breathed in the delightful scents of the grass, the blossoms, and the pine trees of the nearby Radziwill forest. We had no electric light but there was light in our hearts and our eyes sparkled and illuminated the darkness around. We slept soundly and peacefully without fear of burglars or thieves.

On the Sabbath morning, one awakened to the sounds, coming through the open windows, of the chanting of psalms or the reciting of the weekly portion of the Torah. Neither did the women stand idle. They had to wait for the gentile who came to milk the cows on the Sabbath and for the gentile cowherd who took the cows out to pasture. We put on our kapotehs,[4] and girdling cords and our prayer shawls with the tzitzis[5] tucked into the cords, and we walked to the synagogue in whole families, grandfather, father, sons, and grandchildren; a whole regiment!

---

4. A kapoteh is a light overcoat or robe worn for Sabbath and holiday services.
5. Tzitzis are tassels on the corners of prayer shawls.

Later in the day the family would go out for a walk around the fields and gardens to see and take pleasure in the way all was sprouting, growing, and blooming. Many would stroll in the Radziwill forest.[6] The children would pick wild berries with their mouths, for it was forbidden on the Sabbath to pick by hand because that was defined as work.

After the walk, the men would go to the synagogue for the afternoon prayers and would return home to "shalosh seudos," the third meal, a good "borsht"[7] whipped with cream, and again the singing of the zmires[8] would resound throughout Trochenbrod. After evening prayers, we prayed "havdala," which differentiated between a holiday and a routine day. The women then went off to the cow stalls to milk the cows and churn the butter, as it had to be ready for dispatch to Lutsk early on Sunday morning.

---

Shmilike Drossner was a Trochenbroder who also immigrated to the United States before World War I. David Shwartz mentioned him in the excerpt from his memoir in Chapter One. In the 1970s, Shmilike described to an interviewer the traditions in Trochenbrod around each of the Jewish holidays the town celebrated. The interviewer faithfully wrote down what Shmilike said, word for word.

---

6. The Radziwill Forest was on the east side of Trochenbrod. It was owned by a member of the famous Lithuanian and Polish Radziwill family. The Radziwills owned huge tracts of forest land and had lumber interests throughout the Jewish Pale of Settlement.
7. Borsht is a cold beet soup.
8. Zmires means Sabbath songs.

## *The* LOST TOWN

When you read Shmilike's descriptions you can hear him talking. Here is what he had to say about Hanukah, the Festival of Lights:

> I will tell you how we lit our candles on Hanukah in Trochenbrod, and you will think it is funny. We took ordinary potatoes, and cut them in half. We made a small hole in each half, we put a little oil and a piece of cotton in the hole, and then we lit it. The rich probably had candles, but the average person did not have candles and used potatoes instead. The traditions of handing out Hanukah gelt[9] and playing with dreidles[10] was the same as in this country. Also, the tradition of making all kinds of latkes.[11] This was really a treat, and a lot of work supplying the latkes as everyone had good appetites and were not on diets.

 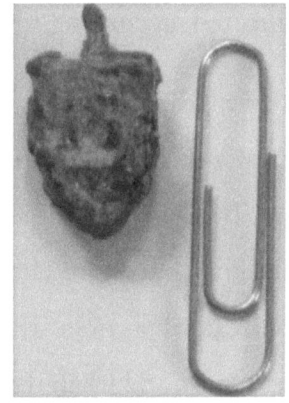

MINIATURE DREIDLE, ABOUT THE WIDTH OF A PAPER CLIP, FOUND IN TROCHENBROD, 2012.
*Recovered by Ivan Podziubanchuk; photographs by the author.*

---

9. Hanukah gelt refers to coins given to children during the Hanukah holiday.
10. Dreidles are spinning tops used for Hanukah games.
11. Latkes are potato pancakes, a traditional Hanukah dish.

About Sukkot or Sukkos, the Feast of Tabernacles, the holiday where Jewish families build a small, temporary hut for eating outdoors to celebrate the fall harvest, Shmilike explained:

> Everybody had a sukkah[12] which they made with their own hands. But our grandfather, Yuda Meir, had one that was sort of stationary, and when Sukkos came, we only had to put the finishing touches on it. Most of the time we froze in there, because the cold weather started earlier in Trochenbrod than here. Some of the sukkahs were made from corn stalks and were so frail that some of the animals, like the cows, would push in the walls. In spite of all this, we enjoyed the holiday.

Baking matzah, the unleavened flatbread eaten during Passover, was complicated, according to Shmilike:

> I want to explain how matzahs were baked in Trochenbrod. The Trochenbroders rented a house in the town for four weeks before Passover. Then they cleaned it thoroughly to make sure it was kosher, and they hired girls and women to make the matzah. One man took care of the oven. Then each family brought flour enough for their family, and when that family's matzah supply was baked, it was delivered to them carried in a bag made of linen hanging from a long pole. And so on, one family after the last one until they had baked enough for everybody. This isn't as simple as it may seem. The water that was used in mixing the flour for the next day

---

12. The sukkah is a temporary hut built and occupied as part of the Sukkot holiday observance.

was brought in before it got dark and put in a barrel overnight. It was brought up from a well, one bucket at a time.

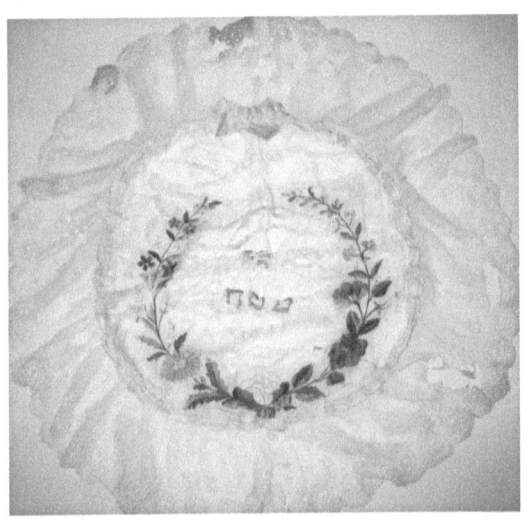

MATZAH COVER MADE BY ELKE ANTWARG, TROCHENBROD, 1913.
*Photograph provided by Miriam Antwarg Ciocler, Elke's granddaughter.*

---

Morris (Moshe) Wolfson came to America in 1912. His father, Wolf, a Trochenbrod shoemaker, had immigrated a few years earlier. David Shwartz also mentioned Wolf in the memoir excerpt in Chapter One. During immigration procedures, the immigration officer asked Morris for his father's name, meaning the family name. Morris misunderstood, and replied, "I'm Wolf's son." The immigration officer wrote "Wolfson" on the immigration form, and that became Morris's legal family name. In 1974, Morris's granddaughter asked him to tell her about life in Trochenbrod, and she turned what he told her into a college essay. A cousin of the granddaughter eventually passed the essay on to me. Here is how Morris Wolfson described life in Trochenbrod in the early 1900s:

> Every day in Trochenbrod, my father, Wolf Shuster,[13] labored over the shoes he made, and every second week he went the twelve miles to the regional market in Kivertzy, where he sold his shoes to gentiles. My family owned a cow that gave us milk. The cow, chickens, ducks, and produce from the vegetable garden made us almost self-sufficient. Every house had a garden that stretched back to the woods.
>
> The 300 or more Jewish families of Trochenbrod (there were no gentiles in our town) lived almost completely separate from the Christians. The train that stopped twelve miles from our town was our only way to reach faraway places, but this was a luxury few could afford. One of my earliest memories was my first time out of our town when I was about four years old. I was sick, and since we did not have a doctor in our town, I was taken on a train ride to Kiev to see one there.
>
> Every boy in Trochenbrod attended kheder[14] from ages four through thirteen. Starting in the early morning, we sat and studied Jewish books all day on hard benches made from wood. We didn't come home until after dark. We studied Hebrew, the Talmud, things like that.
>
> Even though our studies and household chores and learning our father's trade made us grow up quickly, we still had a childhood.

---

13. A shuster is a shoemaker.
14. A kheder is a small Jewish day school, often held in the teacher's house.

Our toys were simple homemade toys. We used to play in the fields. For example, we would make a certain kind of little trap and set it in the field to catch birds. Of course, we would hold the bird and then let it fly away.

In our town, we spoke Yiddish. To the gentiles, we spoke Russian and Polish. Probably more Polish. Trochenbrod was so close to the border, many villages in the area had Polish-speaking peasants. We used the languages of the gentiles when we did business with them.

A wedding was a joyous event in Trochenbrod; everyone participated. Two fathers would meet in the field. "If I'm not mistaken," one says, "you have a girl sixteen years old and my boy's seventeen. I think they would be alright." After deciding on a dowry, which could be money or food and board at the bride's parents' house for a certain amount of time, the fathers shook hands and this way decided their children's fate. At the wedding, everyone danced, men with men and women with women. Meanwhile, the nervous bride and groom sat at the ends of the long table and looked at each other wondering what would be. Despite what each one thought, the match was accepted. There were no Tzeitels, no refusals, and no Chavas, no inter-marriages.[15] Not in our town.

Until I was ten years old, when they used to say the word Jerusalem, or Yerushalaim, I had no idea that it even existed in this world even though I went to kheder. I thought it was something on top of a mountain in heaven.

---

15. Tzeitel and Chava were two of Tevye's daughters in the show, *Fiddler on the Roof*. Tzeitel longed for a different groom than her parents had chosen, and Chava married a gentile.

The only outside thing that everyone knew about was America, the land of opportunity. We were aware only that things were good in America. Everybody wanted to get out and go there where everyone did alright. We thought that the sidewalks were made of gold. America was our goal and how to get there was our major problem.

---

As Europe moved toward World War I, which started in 1914, Trochenbrod was faring well. Its non-agricultural businesses were prospering, and its agricultural activities had spread out to include a wide variety of crops and livestock. While the main crop and staple of the Trochenbrod diet was potatoes, as it had always been, now Trochenbrod farmers also grew wheat, rye, oats, barley, and a variety of vegetables—cabbage, radishes, carrots, cucumbers, beans, corn, tomatoes, and beets. Trochenbroders raised cows for milk and other dairy products, and chickens, geese, and ducks for food, for cooking fat, and for feathers to make pillows and bedding. The nearby forests provided blueberries, red currants, and huckleberries, as they still do today. Because Trochenbrod families lived on the land, they always had enough to eat.

Despite Trochenbrod's relative prosperity in the late 1800s and early 1900s, for many people there were good reasons to go to America if they could. Stories of unbelievable opportunity in America trickled back. Meanwhile, young married people could not set up homes with farms like their forefathers had done because

*The* LOST TOWN

WALL CLOCK CRAFTED BY MICHAL ANTWARG, TROCHENBROD, 1914.
*Photograph provided by Miriam Antwarg Ciocler, Michal's granddaughter.*

no more farmland was available in Trochenbrod; some found farmland in the sister village of Lozisht, but others emigrated. Although Trochenbrod's location in the forest had shielded it from anti-Jewish gangs so far, reports of pogroms across Russia meant that there would probably be trouble ahead. Also, Czarist anti-Jewish regulations were still in effect, so there was little hope for Jews to enjoy a comfortable future in Russia. Finally, Trochenbrod's young men were threatened with being drafted into the Czar's army during the Russo-Japanese war in 1904 and 1905. A great wave of these young men found ways to escape and immigrate to North and South America. Trochenbrod immigrants who went to America settled in larger cities like New York, Boston, Baltimore, Cleveland,

Columbus, Pittsburgh, Detroit, Philadelphia, Washington, DC, and Portsmouth.

ENGAGEMENT PHOTO OF ELKE AND MICHAL ANTWARG, TROCHENBROD, 1913.
*Photograph provided by Miriam Antwarg Ciocler.*

---

Rabbi Mosheh-David Pearlmutter came from the town of Verba, about 65 miles south of Trochenbrod. Mosheh-David's father had been a rabbi in Verba; they were descended from a long line of rabbis well-known in that region. In 1910, word came that a rabbi in Trochenbrod had died, and people from his synagogue wanted to know if Mosheh-David would agree to replace him. Mosheh-David jumped at the opportunity to be a rabbi in a town where being a

Jew meant being what everyone else was. He gathered his family and household goods and moved to Trochenbrod. Rabbi Pearlmutter's synagogue was located near the south end of Trochenbrod. He moved into the house next door with his wife, Beila, and their eight children. They settled in, and soon Rabbi Mosheh-David Pearlmutter was one of Trochenbrod's highly respected rabbis. In 1912, Beila gave birth to a son they named YomTov—holiday, a day of happiness. They chose this name because they had not expected to be blessed with another child. In order to record their new son as first-born so that later he would not be drafted into the Russian Army, Rabbi Mosheh-David, my grandfather, changed the family name. He became Rabbi Mosheh-David Beider. Thirty years later, YomTov Beider became my father. Everyone knew him as YomTov Beider from Trochenbrod.

When YomTov Beider was just two years old, World War I broke out. As Austrian troops pushed into Russia, and then the Russian troops pushed back, there was widespread destruction in the area around Trochenbrod. The glass factory and several other small factories were destroyed in the fighting; livestock were taken by the army; soldiers broke into homes and shops and stole goods, furniture, and personal property; and mail stopped arriving. People often emigrated with the idea of bringing the rest of their family when they had enough money. In the meantime, they would send money home to support their family. Now money could not arrive. The economy of Trochenbrod was destroyed; the people were terrorized and brutalized by the soldiers.

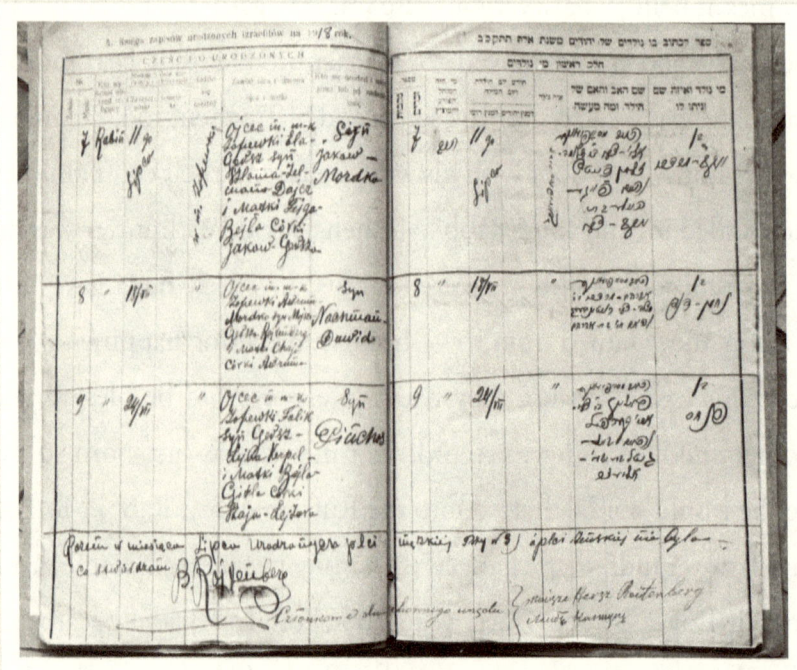

SOFIYOVKA BIRTH RECORDS, 1918.
THE LEFT SIDE IS IN POLISH, THE RIGHT SIDE IN HEBREW.
*Record book found in the State Archive of the Volyn Region, Lutsk, Ukraine.*

Under the Russians in 1914, Cossacks[16] had been allowed to ransack Trochenbrod, pillaging, raping, and murdering. When the Austrians pushed the Russians out and occupied Trochenbrod in 1915, they at first collected all the food to feed their troops and gave back only scraps to the townspeople. They required everyone to cook, wash, sew, make leather goods, tend horses, or in some other way support the army, even on the Sabbath.

During the nine months of Austrian occupation, Rabbi Beider made a special effort to be friendly with the Austrian commander

---

16. Cossacks were a militaristic ethnic group with their own culture. They were loyal to Russia and treated Jews with special cruelty.

and gain his confidence. He spent long evenings discussing world events in German with the commander, and eventually they became friends. Rabbi Beider convinced the commander that the people of Trochenbrod could produce more for the Austrian Army if the commander would allow them to observe the Sabbath and Jewish holidays, have a more reasonable workload at other times, and eat better food. As a result of this, conditions became much better in Trochenbrod, and Trochenbrod's Jews remembered both Rabbi Beider and the Austrian commander with great respect for many years.

The devastation of World War I put a sudden end to the steady growth in prosperity that Trochenbrod enjoyed before the war. It put a sudden end to Trochenbrod/Sofiyovka's expanding role as the center of economic activity in the region. It changed Trochenbrod from a strong and proud little town to a place where there was nothing but poverty and misery.

―――

Shaindeleh Gluz[17] was born in Trochenbrod in 1913, exactly 100 years after the first baby was born there. In 2002, she wrote her memoir about life in her hometown so that her grandchildren and their children would not forget Trochenbrod. A relative passed the memoir to me in 2008. Here is how Shaindeleh described her life during the period of World War I:

---

17. The name Gluz comes from the word "glass"; people in that family were glassworkers.

Grandma and some of her family left for America in 1914. There was a lot of unrest in the world. There were rumors of war, and suddenly it happened; World War I was on. There was no way to escape. Immigration was stopped, there was no mail, no communication . . . only pain and suffering. The invading army confiscated money, jewels, silver and all valuables from the town's people. When the war was finally over, all the plundering and killing stopped. People came out of hiding, no more attacks, no more rapes, no more deaths of innocent people. My grandfather's home had been stripped of all furnishings that had been in the family for generations, but we were alive. The war took its toll on my parents, especially my mother. She was very sick. She was always in bed. Our clothes were torn and neglected. There was little food in the house. Mother was too weak to improvise any meals with the little bits of scraps that we had. Most of the time my little brother Yossel and I stayed in bed with Mother to keep warm, but we were so hungry. Once in a while, while in bed with Mother, Yossel and I would play a game, Let's Pretend, with a large collection of well-worn colorful picture postcards. The cards were of the Statue of Liberty and the teaming Lower East Side of New York. Mother's family sent the cards to us when they settled in America. From these pictures, Mother would weave wonderful tales of freedom, peace, happiness and plenty. Shortly after Mother passed away, many more sad happenings began. My little brother Yossel and my father became very ill. One morning my little brother's body was cold and stiff. He had died of smallpox. I suppose that

*The* LOST TOWN

Yossel's death really caused father's complete breakdown, and then his death. There came a time when we really didn't have a piece of bread to eat. We foraged in the woods for berries and sour grass. Our bellies became swollen. We found ourselves too weak from hunger, too sick with festering body sores and lice to give a care anymore. Make no mistake; we were not alone in this situation. All of Trochenbrod was suffering. We became like animals, hunting for scraps of food and struggling to survive. Just when the struggle became too much to bear . . . Since the war was finally over, traveling was again possible, and the first person to arrive in Trochenbrod was a rich American. He had been commissioned by relatives in America to go to our town and seek out their relatives. He brought letters and money for some of the people. He was also asked to help some of the townspeople to make their way to America. My brother and I ran and reached the center of town just in time to hear the American call out our names.

---

When all the fighting was finished, Trochenbrod found itself in a different country. About 150 years earlier, before Russia took over the area in which Trochenbrod would be created, that region had been a part of Poland. Poland had now recaptured some of its ancient land, and the people of Trochenbrod/Sofiyovka, which since its beginning had known only the rule of Russian Czars, looked around and discovered that now they were citizens of Poland.

My father, YomTov Beider, as a Jewish pioneer, Palestine, 1933.
*Photographer unknown; photograph found in an old scrapbook long after YomTov's death.*

CHAPTER THREE

# Booming Between The Wars

## 1920s

I was lucky to fall under Trochenbrod's spell at a time when numbers of people, both Jewish and gentile, who knew the town from personal experience were still alive. Once I had resolved to learn Trochenbrod's history and what it was like to live in this all-Jewish town, I flew as fast as I could arrange to interview people born in Trochenbrod who now lived all around America and in Brazil, Israel, Poland, and Ukraine. Among the Jewish people I interviewed, some had left Trochenbrod when they were as young as five years old; others had left when they were young adults, like my father; and others were Holocaust survivors. Almost all the Jewish people I interviewed were born in Trochenbrod in the period from 1920, just after World War I, through 1932.

Almost all the Ukrainians and Poles I interviewed came from the surrounding villages. They knew Trochenbrod because they had gone to the public school there or because they had visited the town with their parents who shopped and did business there. A few said they developed childhood friends in Trochenbrod because of the school.

The people I interviewed told me stories about life in Trochenbrod in the 20-year period between World War I and World War II. When I heard these stories, I realized they were the kinds of stories my father might have told me because that's the period when he was maturing into a young man who was very active in many aspects of Trochenbrod life.

Though their stories differed slightly, I felt they were reliable. It reminded me of hearing different descriptions of a trip from friends who vacationed together. One way I tried to sort through the different accounts was to ask everyone I interviewed about some of the same things—the types of work gentiles from neighboring villages did for Trochenbrod businesses and families, for example—and then compared the answers. I also videotaped everyone I interviewed. That way I could see and hear exactly what each person had said, and whether they had said it with conviction or perhaps with a hint of uncertainty, and I could review it again and again. It was also possible, in many cases, to compare what people I interviewed had said against relevant documents or even photographs.

For example, many people told me that Trochenbrod had a large number and wide variety of retail shops and artisanal workshops. Everyone could name a few of the shops and workshops, but no one could be specific about what was a "large number" or a "wide variety." They were describing how it seemed and what it felt like to them; but that wasn't enough to bring Trochenbrod alive for other people. I started looking for documents and discovered a Polish business directory that not only listed all the businesses in Trochenbrod in 1929 but also the family names of the owners. This enabled me to confirm or build detail around facts I had heard from people I had interviewed.

RABBI MOSHE HIRSCH ROITENBERG, TROCHENBROD, MID-1930S.
*Copied from* Hailan V'shoreshav *(The Tree and Its Roots), Bet Tal, Israel, 1988.*

To have their pictures taken, Trochenbroders often went to Lutsk, a large city about 20 miles away—close to a day's journey—for studio photographs. But sometimes traveling photographers would arrive in Trochenbrod and set up temporary studios, and many people would have portraits of their families made there. This explains why you can look through hundreds of photographs from Trochenbrod and see the faces of its people, often stiff and posed, but see nothing of what the town looked like.

By the 1930s, people in America and Western Europe had box cameras and 35 mm cameras. Some visitors to Trochenbrod, usually immigrants who came back to see their families, snapped outdoor photos. Some Trochenbroders had cameras, too, but their photographs perished as they did in the Holocaust. The one Trochenbroder who took outdoor photographs in the town and survived the Holocaust with her photographs and other personal belongings was the Catholic postmistress Polish authorities had sent to the town—Janina Lubinski. I met her son, Ryszard Lubinski, in the city of Radom, two hours away by car from Warsaw, Poland's capital city. Ryszard gave me most of the photos of 1930s' Trochenbrod that appear in this book. They were taken by his mother, a technology enthusiast who was ahead of her time. These photographs offer wonderful glimpses the town my father grew up in.

*The* LOST TOWN

When my father marked his Bar Mitzva in the early 1920s, the population of Trochenbrod together with its sister village Lozisht was the same as it had been 20 years earlier—about 1,600 people. Any natural growth had been offset by emigration and death from disease, hunger, exhaustion, and sickness caused by World War I.

The first few years after World War I and the shorter Polish-Soviet War that followed[18] were a period of harsh life and recovery. In the early days of Polish administration, local military commanders put Trochenbrod Jewish men on forced labor crews. Without pay, these crews had to build roads and government buildings; make food, clothes, and leather goods for the Polish Army; haul construction materials and army supplies; and build furniture for Polish government offices. As things settled down and the military administration was replaced with a civilian administration, government-level anti-Semitic policies were put in place. Government jobs could not be held by Jews. Some businesses in which Jews had played major roles, like selling vodka and salt, were declared state monopolies and turned over to Polish-Catholic war veterans to operate. Anti-Semitism, anti-Semitic practices, and violence against Jews increased steadily in Poland in the 20 years between World War I and World War II.

But people in the rural areas tended to get along better than in the cities—Poles, Ukrainians, and Jews each had their own villages and economic roles, and they all needed each other. Despite the

---

18. In a large region that included Trochenbrod, World War I was followed immediately by a two-year conflict over borders between Poland and the Soviet Union (which had replaced Russia during World War I), in which Poland was victorious. As a result, the place where Trochenbrod stood became a part of Eastern Poland until World War II.

government's ant-Semitic policies, Trochenbrod's economy again grew and reached into a wide variety of non-agricultural activities.

The war pushed Trochenbrod on a faster path to modernization. During World War I, Trochenbrod had rubbed up against soldiers and their commanders from four different countries—Russia, Austria, Poland, and the Soviet Union. These exposed Trochenbrod's people to different languages, cultures, equipment, machines, values, ideas, and ideologies. In that period, young men who had fled to distant cities to avoid the troubles in Trochenbrod or attend yeshivas, now returned to Trochenbrod more knowledgeable about the world outside. Some young men had been taken into the military where they were exposed to a secular world, modern military machinery, political ideas, and unkosher food—and they talked about what they had seen and experienced when they returned to Trochenbrod.

During the 20 years between World War I and World War II, Trochenbrod and its people became steadily more worldly, modern, secular, and political. By 1925, Trochenbrod had taken a proverbial deep breath, and its people had figured out how to deal with its new ruler, the Polish government. Trochenbroders understood the town didn't need more agricultural land in order to thrive in the modern world. Trochenbrod reasserted itself as the commercial center for the rural region surrounding it, and as the 1920s gave way to the 1930s, Trochenbrod grew rapidly again. Trochenbrod had its tailors, teachers, carpenters, blacksmiths, locksmiths, painters, brick makers, bricklayers, foresters, and wheelwrights. It had sawmills and even a glue factory. Its economy was more and more becoming the trade, crafts, agro-processing, and light manufacturing center for a region stretching 10 to 15 miles around the town.

## 1930s

When entrepreneurial Trochenbroders encountered a good business opportunity—as they often did when they traded with the surrounding villages—they seized and built on it.

Avrum Bass was a good example of a man who was both a farmer and a city entrepreneur. A farmer who had a horse and wagon to carry his produce to regional markets, Avrum would often bring produce back from the market in his wagon to sell in Trochenbrod. He soon became as much a produce trader as a farmer. As his produce trading business grew, he needed a stronger horse, so he sold the one he had and bought another. He saw that he had made a good trade and decided to buy another horse and trade that one. Before long, he was regularly buying and selling horses—without planning it, he had also become a horse trader. Sometimes he brought bread back from the market to sell. Why not bake it here, he thought, and offer fresher bread that people from the nearby villages might also come to buy?

Soon enough Avrum Bass was a well-to-do businessman who grew and traded produce, was a trader in horses, and owned a busy bakery in Trochenbrod.

Dairy owners took their milk and butter to Lutsk, Rovno, and Kolki to sell. Why come back with empty wagons? they probably thought. The dairy owners bought sugar, cooking oil, and eventually a wide variety of other goods from the cities to resell at home. They expanded their dairy shops into grocery stores. Soon they thought of themselves not just as dairymen, but also grocery shopkeepers and traders in city goods.

Earlier in this book, I mentioned that even in the early days some Trochenbroders raised cattle to supplement their income from crops and gradually developed businesses in dairy products and leather and leather products. The leather business was a big business—the biggest business—in Trochenbrod, with dairy products being second. The leather business included buying cows for their skins; buying skins for tanning; tanning operations, which turned the skins into leather; and working the leather into various products, especially boots and shoes. Then there were leather goods shops, shoe shops, and shoe repair shops. Trochenbrod's leather business also included exporting leather and leather goods to cities in the area, trading leather goods at regional markets, selling from wagons of leather merchandise village-by-village, and selling wholesale to small shops in other villages. There were about forty leather-related businesses in Trochenbrod by the late 1930s. In addition, many families had tools in their homes for leather working on a small scale.

POSTMISTRESS JANINA LUBINSKI IN FRONT OF TROCHENBROD'S POST OFFICE.
ELI POTASH, PARTIALLY SEEN, ON THE STEPS OF HIS LEATHER WORKSHOP NEXT DOOR,
MID-1930S.
*Photographer unknown; photograph provided by Ryszard Lubinski, Janina's son.*

Eli Potash had started out making shoes and selling them in his small shop like so many other Trochenbroders. To get more business, he bought a horse and wagon and made rounds in the villages to take orders for new shoes. His customers would ask him for other leather goods, like belts and bridles. Steadily he expanded his leather "export" business. By the mid-1930s, Eli had a large leather workshop in its own building next to the post office, where he and his workers made a wide variety of leather products for a steady market of customers in the villages around Trochenbrod. He made a good living from this and was able to build a very nice new house.

Eli could not have imagined that just a few years later, his house would be selected by Nazi officers for a place to live and to store the possessions of their victims, while Eli and his family struggled to survive the winter hiding in the Radziwill Forest.

---

In 1929, there was an entry for Sofiyovka, now the official Polish name for Trochenbrod, in *Księga Adresowa Polski*, a privately published Polish business directory. The entry listed about 90 businesses in Sofiyovka, everything from barber shops and bakeries, to pharmacies and fabric shops, to oil presses and flour mills.

Many prominent Trochenbrod family names show up there as owners of the enterprises—names that today are spread throughout North and South America and Israel, and also throughout this book:

| | |
|---|---|
| Antwarg | Kerman |
| Blitsztein | Kessler |
| Bulmash | Potash |
| Burak | Roitenberg |
| Drossner | Safran |
| Fishfader | Schuster |
| Gelman | Shpielman |
| Gilden | Shwartz |
| Gluz | Szames |
| Halperin | Wainer |

In addition to the Trochenbrod businesses listed in *Księga Adresowa Polski*, Trochenbroders provided services like house building, window repairing, carpentry, painting, brick-laying, roofing, and other craft specialties to people in the surrounding villages. They even operated branches of their stores in nearby villages. As the years passed, Trochenbrod became more and more a major commercial center, a regional town, a town that everyone—Jews and gentiles alike—were certain would one day become a city.

---

The very first time I visited the Trochenbrod area, as we were trying to locate the site of the town, we saw an aged woman bent over, working, in the fields of a neighboring village called Domashiv. Through our Ukrainian guide, we asked if she could point us toward the site of Sofiyovka.

She slowly straightened up from her hoeing and first looked at us sternly, as if wondering, Who is this asking me such things? But then, when she realized we were foreigners, the features of her weathered face softened into a smile. She twisted and pointed, "There," she said. "Keep walking in that direction through the fields on the other side of those trees, and you'll see a small black monument that marks the north end of Sofiyovka. If there had been no German Nazis, you wouldn't need to ask, because you'd see it. It would be a city today, bigger than Lutsk."

An interesting idea. Might Trochenbrod really have become a city—big stone buildings, a subway system, a network of paved streets with sidewalks, cars everywhere, a railroad station, fancy restaurants and shops—a completely Jewish city, a Tel Aviv in Ukraine? Why not? Everyone today might know it as, say, the center of high technology or app development or e-business in Ukraine. It would have high-speed links to Kiev and New York and Tel Aviv. And at the same time, everyone would know that if you want the best gefilte fish in Ukraine, Trochenbrod—Sofiyovka—was the place to go.

Despite its rapid growth in the 1930s, its prosperity, and its modernization, Trochenbrod remained, after all, Trochenbrod. It was still surrounded by forests, far from any reliable transportation route that automobiles could use; and if you sniffed the air of Trochenbrod, you smelled the soil and crops and livestock of farming. Many of its houses had been improved and enlarged. Many of the shops now had their own storefronts and carried a steadily increasing variety of goods. The families lived in back. However, Trochenbrod was still one long street with houses, shops, workshops, small factories, and synagogues. But now, public buildings like schools, a cultural center, the post office, and the constable's office were also lined up along it.

Trochenbrod was still somewhat isolated and completely Jewish—except for the postmistress, policeman, and vodka store operator who had been brought by the Polish government to work there. Despite the fact that it was now a rapidly growing Polish town, it continued to be a town governed by Jewish custom: the people of Trochenbrod continued to observe the Sabbath and Jewish holidays, to keep strictly kosher and to follow Jewish tradition, to fill the town's synagogues, and to greet visiting Jewish scholars with celebrations. For Jews who knew about the town and for most who lived there, the fact that this was a Jewish town, together with its farming character, gave Trochenbrod an out-of-place and out-of-time magical quality.

Because it was so unusual for Jews to be farmers, many from the outside who visited Trochenbrod were struck especially by its farming and country way of life; they hardly noticed that people in Trochenbrod earned most of their living from non-farm activities. A person who later became an Israeli writer once visited Trochenbrod as a young man. His name was Jacob Banai, and this is what he wrote in his 1978 book, *Anonymous Soldiers*:

> Sofiyovka was the name of a small Polish town in which in the fall of 1938 the first Etzel[19] course took place, in which I participated. The Jews led their lives in Sofiyovka as if it was their kingdom. That is where I first encountered Jews who worked in agriculture. In Sofiyovka I saw Jews walking behind their plows; a Jew who takes his cows to the field, and when the time for prayer has arrived he stands in his field and prays as if he is standing in a synagogue.
>
> That picture deeply ingrained itself in my memory, and it was the first taste I had of our vision of a Jew in his homeland. I also saw children there, not organized in any activities, but actually small children playing in the fields, dancing and singing Hebrew songs. What a magical place was this Sofiyovka!

---

19. Etzel was a Jewish military organization that trained to fight for a Jewish state in Palestine.

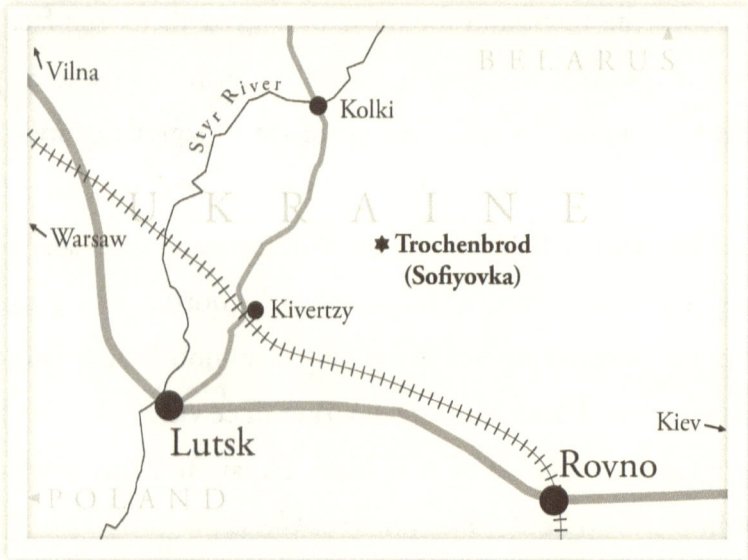

TROCHENBROD AND THE SURROUNDING AREA, MID-1930S.
*Map by Alan Pranke.*

By the mid-1930s, the Polish government began improving transportation in the area. The road from the Kivertzy railroad station to Lutsk was paved, and there was bus service between the cities of Lutsk, Rovno, and Kolki. Many Trochenbroders now traveled often to the cities of the region. Basia-Ruchel Potash, Eli Potash's daughter, was a child growing up in Trochenbrod in the 1930s. She remembers having feelings like those of country girls everywhere when they set eyes on the big city:

> I liked to go with my father when he went to the big city, Lutsk, when he went to buy leather and things. He would take me along. I'd look at the buildings and the people and the shop windows and the cars; it was so exciting! I dreamt, "When I grow up, that's what I'm going to do. I'm going to live in the big city."

ZIONIST SUMMER CAMP, TROCHENBROD, 1939.
*Photograph by Janina Lubinski; provided by Ryszard Lubinski.*

---

The population of Trochenbrod and Lozisht grew from 1,600 people at the beginning of the 1920s to 5,000 near the end of the 1930s. Population growth brought with it an explosion in the number of young people in the town. Because Trochenbrod had more contact with the outside world, these young people were exposed to Zionism—to the idea of building a Jewish homeland in Palestine. Zionism took strong hold in Trochenbrod, as it did among young Jews throughout Eastern Europe in this period. Many of Trochenbrod's young people joined Zionist organizations, and these organizations represented all the different Zionist political views, from the militaristic-individualistic to the agricultural-communal. The strongest Zionist youth group in Trochenbrod was Beitar, which believed in Jewish military strength and self-defense.

Even Ryszard Lubinski, son of the Catholic postmistress, and the only gentile born in Trochenbrod, was close to Beitar. In one interview, he told me:

> There were Jewish organizations in Trochenbrod, and sometimes they fought among themselves. Do you know of an organization called Beitar? I was close to the people in that organization. The head of it was someone named Anshel Shpielman. That organization wanted to fight for Palestine, for a Jewish state in Palestine. The other organizations wanted to negotiate for land and that caused some conflict among them.

Trochenbrod's Zionist groups met regularly. They had educational programs, sometimes separately and sometimes in cooperation; they put on plays; they held evenings of Hebrew music and dance; they conducted special holiday celebrations; they encouraged the use of modern conversational Hebrew; and they sent more than a hundred Jewish "pioneers" to Palestine in the 1920s and 1930s. One of the basic principles of all the Zionist youth groups was returning to the Hebrew language, which would be the language of the new Jewish State. By the mid-1930s, the language of Trochenbrod, Yiddish, had been joined by modern Hebrew as a language used in some homes and public meetings. Formal and informal Hebrew language classes were everywhere. Trochenbrod, that little isolated town in the midst of Ukrainian villages and forests, even produced poets and authors who published their work in both Hebrew and Yiddish. My uncle, whose short poems appear in Chapters 4 and 8, was one of them.

---

A point of pride among native Trochenbroders is that in 1938, the first training course outside Palestine for Etzel officers was conducted in Trochenbrod, as Jacob Banai has written. Etzel was an early Jewish nationalist organization associated with the Beitar Zionist youth group. Menachim Begin, who fought the British in Palestine and later became Prime Minister of Israel, had been an Etzel leader. Trochenbrod offered the leaders of Etzel a special set of conditions for their military training: it was relatively remote from the eyes of Polish authorities; it provided a rural environment with both open land and forest land good for military training; most of its youth were solidly behind the Zionist cause; and it was a Jewish town that would support the training with enthusiasm.

Alongside the Zionist excitement in Trochenbrod, Jewish religious observance, tradition, and scholarship continued to be strong. All young men and women I spoke with who had lived in Trochenbrod during the 1930s had been Zionists, but the men also had been yeshiva students. They had studied both in nearby towns and in major cities far away, like Warsaw.

Trochenbrod had many synagogues in the mid-1930s—some Trochenbroders told me that as many as nine operated at the same time in Trochenbrod and Lozisht. Everyone in Trochenbrod

THE "TALMUD TORAH" (BOYS-ONLY) JEWISH DAY SCHOOL, 1939.
*Photographer unknown; many people in Israel and the United States provided copies of this photograph. It also appears in* Hailan V'shoreshav *(The Tree and Its Roots), Bet Tal, Israel, 1988.*

followed Orthodox Jewish law and customs. As one Trochenbroder put it, "You were either an Orthodox Jew or they called you a goy."[20]

Trochenbroders who were youngsters in the 1930s talked about the Sabbath using the same words as those who remembered Sabbaths in Trochenbrod 50 years earlier. It was a day for which everyone prepared by baking khallah[21] and special chulunt dishes;[22] bathing; cleaning their houses; sending the children door-to-door collecting baked goods to give to the poor; and dressing appropriately for greeting and being in the company of "the Sabbath Queen," an affectionate name for the special Sabbath day. There were always

---

20. Goy is the Hebrew word for "nation" and is used in this instance to mean gentile.
21. Khallah is braided egg-bread.
22. Chulunt dishes are stews that simmer all day over a low fire.

guests for the Sabbath, often merchants visiting Trochenbrod who could not get home before the start of the holy day, on which travel was forbidden. Everyone happily brought a guest from Friday night prayers to share dinner and their home for the Sabbath. Sabbath was a day of peace, rest, prayer, family, good eating, socializing, strolling in the Radziwill Forest, Sabbath songs, and pausing to enjoy the goodness that God, hard work, and Trochenbrod provided.

For a Bar Mitzva in Trochenbrod, the family offered a piece of sponge cake, some fruit, and a taste of schnapps, a kind of whiskey, for the men after prayers. Weddings, however, were a different matter. Much of the town showed up for the outdoor ceremony. Children recited poems and sang songs, and one of the women baked a huge khallah and danced while holding it before the bride and groom. It was a time to forget everything else and rejoice. The bride and groom performed their marriage rituals under the chuppah, the wedding canopy. A klezmer trio, a band of Jewish folk musicians, was brought in from Kolki and played enthusiastically for the feast that followed—Tzalik beat the symbols and drums, Peshi with a big white beard played the fiddle, and Khaim's fingers danced wildly on the clarinet. There was nothing like a Trochenbrod wedding!

---

In the late 1920s, Prince Janush Radziwill, the owner of the forest on the east side of Trochenbrod, built a Catholic church at the edge of his forest, near the northern end of town. It served about 30 Polish families who lived along a forest trail just south of Trochenbrod. No one knows why he built the church exactly in that location, but it resulted in a large group of Poles walking the full length of Trochenbrod's muddy street on their way to and from church every Sunday. They dressed in their go-to-church finest clothes, almost as if they were taking a stroll in the city of Lutsk, with their priest at the head of the crowd.

POLISH CATHOLIC CHURCHGOERS WALK THROUGH TROCHENBROD ON A SUNDAY MORNING, 1930s.
*Photograph by Janina Lubinski; provided by Ryszard Lubinski.*

This was described to me by Trochenbroders who witnessed it as children in the 1930s. As the strolling church groups passed through town, young men in the groups would sometimes strike at townspeople just to show who was boss. Others remember the Poles going to church through town as a good thing because while walking through town, churchgoers often stopped in a Trochenbrod shop to buy something.

Peshia Gotman, who was born in Trochenbrod and grew up there into her teen years, told me that she remembered the church most of all as a source of excitement:

> I remember that church, and how! My mother gave me a good beating because I ran to be at the "otpus"—it's when they have their services outside. It's like a big picnic. It's some kind of ceremony. I was maybe ten years old. I was with a whole bunch of kids. They usually had ice cream and all kinds of toys; the whole church was having a picnic outside! I got a big spanking for that because I was not supposed to go to the church.

I wonder what Prince Radziwill was thinking? Did he deliberately locate the church so there would be a procession of Catholic worshippers right through Trochenbrod every Sunday, and to give Trochenbrod people a good view of the church and events in the churchyard? Was he thinking that Trochenbroders might even want to go to the church and eventually convert, or perhaps it would make Trochenbrod's children want to go to the church's "otpuses"? Trochenbroders I interviewed had different views but all agreed the weekly church processions stood out in the life of this all-Jewish town.

By the mid-1930s, many Trochenbroders who had immigrated to America before World War I were returning to visit family who had stayed. Sometimes they would to try to convince their

Trochenbrod relatives to leave because they were worried about Hitler and the terrible things Germany might do. Hitler became the most powerful man in Germany in 1933. In 1934, he signed a non-aggression treaty with Poland that encouraged even greater anti-Semitism there. But other than the occasional Sunday brawl with Polish churchgoers, Trochenbrod had not been directly affected by anti-Jewish actions and continued to prosper and modernize. Most Trochenbroders thought they had a bright future.

By the late 1930s, Trochenbrod had become *the* place to shop and do business in the region. Many elderly Ukrainians today remember visiting Trochenbrod as children with their parents and being amazed by all that could be bought there. To those children from the surrounding farm villages, the houses of Trochenbroders seemed bigger and better than their own, and the hustle-and-bustle in the street was exciting.

One elderly woman in Horodiche, a village about four miles through the forest southeast of Trochenbrod, told me that as a child she would beg her father to take her with him on his shopping trips to Sofiyovka. For her, it was like going to the big city. A Ukrainian from the village of Yaromel, a village about two miles away, remembered, "Beautiful stores there; lots of different kinds of stores." He also remembered Trochenbrod shopkeepers as gentle and kind people. He told me:

> We bought things there: fabrics, clothes, shoes, and other things.
> If we needed to buy something but we didn't have the money,

the Jewish shopkeepers would say, "Don't worry, it's okay; when you have the money, you'll pay me." They were good people. They trusted everyone.

An old-timer from the nearby village of Domashiv reminisced:

> They hired Ukrainians from nearby villages to work in their fields. Ukrainians from the surrounding villages would go there to try to find something to do to earn money. They could get two zlotys[23] for helping in the fields, and the Trochenbroders would give them a cup of tea. They would even hire Ukrainians to cut their grasses for their cattle because the Trochenbrod people were busy trading. They were selling all sorts of leather goods, and they were buying animals for hides to make leather to make those goods.
>
> Before the war, everyone was friendly. The Jews, Ukrainians, and Poles all had different professions and did business with each other. People from different villages went around to other villages. They might sew clothes or repair something in someone's house. Everyone had his own job, so it was peaceful and friendly, and everyone had his own piece of land and worked on it.

A woman in a nearby Polish village, on what used to be the principal road from Trochenbrod to Kivertzy and Lutsk, knew Trochenbrod and many of its people well. She told me:

> My parents used to take me to Sofiyovka because there were a lot of shops there where we could buy a lot of things. The

---

23. Zlotys are Polish coins.

people from all the villages around Sofiyovka went there to get everything they needed.

We had bees, and we sold honey there in the summer. We took the honey by horse wagon. People came with jars or whatever containers they had, and my grandfather poured the honey into it. We brought the honey in a bucket and strawberries, also, to sell along the street.

Trochenbrod's bustling street, 1939. The girl is Eli Potash's daughter, Basia-Ruchel. The boy is Ryszard Lubinski, son of the postmistress. *Photograph by Janina Lubinski; provided by Ryszard Lubinski.*

---

In the final years of the 1930s, modern technology found its way to Trochenbrod. The first electricity, radios, bicycles, and movies appeared. The Yiddish newspaper, *Forward*, was delivered regularly. Trochenbrod's post office now also offered telephone and telegraph service. Improved roads made travel to the train station at Kivertzy and to Lutsk more routine. The District Administration planted more trees in Trochenbrod; they installed short posts to keep traffic out of the drainage ditches along Trochenbrod's street; and they even started a project to upgrade the street with paving stones because after a rain, the street would become muddy and horse wagons would get stuck.

RIBBON CUTTING FOR THE FIRST (AND ONLY)
PAVED SECTION OF TROCHENBROD'S STREET, 1939.
*Photograph by Janina Lubinski; provided by Ryszard Lubinski.*

The project to pave Trochenbrod's street began in 1938. At that time, Peshia Gotman was a 17-year-old preparing to immigrate to America. She watched the paving work and had second thoughts about leaving:

> To me, Trochenbrod looked like a street that had been picked up
> from a city and plopped down somewhere in the wilderness, except

the street was mud. Seeing the street being paved convinced me that what we all expected was starting to happen—Trochenbrod was going to become a city, a Jewish city. Why would I leave it?

---

In November 1938, Kristallnacht, a night of terrible attacks on synagogues, Jewish-owned shops, and Jewish people, took place in Germany. Kristallnacht means "night of glass." When it was over, shattered glass from Jewish stores and other buildings lay everywhere in the streets of German cities. After Kristallnacht, a terrible storm of hatred began to gather.

Over the next few years, actions against the Jews continued and intensified in Germany until they burst into the horror we call the Holocaust, in which the Nazis and their helpers killed six million Jews and six million other innocent people. Trochenbrod's 5,000 Jews could not imagine that Hitler's Germany was really as bad as people said—and they remembered that the Austrians, who they thought of as "Germans," had treated them relatively well in World War I. Besides, they thought, why would anyone want to bother a pleasant, friendly, and industrious town like Trochenbrod, whose people served everyone in the region well and caused trouble to no one? The ribbon-cutting for the first small paved section of Trochenbrod's street was held in spring 1939. That was the last section ever paved.

On August 23, 1939, Germany and the Soviet Union signed a pact called the Molotov-Ribbentrop Pact in which they promised not to attack each other. The pact included a secret agreement that divided Poland between them: Germany would take Western Poland, and the USSR would take Eastern Poland, which included Trochenbrod. A week later, Germany invaded Poland from the west, and two weeks later the Soviet Union invaded from the east. The Soviet Union took territory it failed to keep in its war with Poland 20 years earlier, after World War I, so Trochenbrod came under Soviet rule once again. World War II had begun.

At that moment, everything began to change. Shmulik Potash (not related to Eli Potash), left Trochenbrod soon after the Soviet Union took control. When I interviewed him, he asked to speak directly to readers of this book about the Trochenbrod he remembered before dusk and then darkness covered it:

> Although there were plenty of poor people in Trochenbrod, they were all wealthy. Why? Because they felt their lives were rich and they were satisfied. There's a saying, "Want what you have, and then you'll have what you want." Ninety-five percent of Trochenbrod people were like that. They were salt of the earth, as they say. The very concept of stealing was unknown to them. Take something that belongs to someone else? What's that?
>
> The people who read your book . . . I want to tell them that there once was a Jewish town of worthy people, hard-working people, honest people, trusting people. All they wanted was to raise children who would also be good people. That's what Trochenbrod was.

## CHAPTER FOUR
# Dusk And Darkness

Within a couple months of their invasion, Nazis began building ghettos in Western Poland, forcing Jews to live in crowded, unsanitary conditions, then starving them, using them as slaves, and eventually taking them to death camps. Most Polish Jews did not understand fully what was being done to them until it was too late or they became helpless to escape their circumstances. But some sensed quickly how grave their situation was and fled as soon as they could—if they could—to other countries or to Eastern Poland, which was occupied by Soviet forces. Some Jews in Western Poland, however, had observed the increasing anti-Semitism and rising sympathy with Nazi ideas among Poles and understood even before the German invasion that their situation was not secure and might soon be disastrous.

## *The* LOST TOWN

The following poem expresses this. I found the poem, originally written in Yiddish, among newspaper clippings my father had saved. It was composed by his brother, Yisrael, and published in 1939 in the *Podlayisher Tzeitung* (Podlayisher Newspaper), in Mezerich, Poland. At the time he composed this poem, most of Yisrael's brothers had immigrated to Palestine, like my father, or to Brazil or America. His wife had recently died, and Yisrael was worried that he may have waited too long to flee with his two children.

ON THE WATER
By Yisrael Beider

My brothers have reached the far shore,
Landed on solid ground.
I alone remain, midway,
My ship heavily burdened.

I was late, thought I could hurry and reach the other side.
But then, night fell.
And who knows how long until day.
Where I stand is not firm, it's like froth on the water.

I see a little star,
A sparkling from far away.
My brothers are sending greetings to me.
Their flame burns there on the other side.

## Soviet Rule

For this brief era in Trochenbrod's history, I was able to interview a number of people, both Jews and gentiles, who had witnessed all or part of it. All of them had remarkable stories to tell, as you might expect from people who escaped or lived through the Holocaust. Their first-person accounts are treasures for the insight they provide into what happened and what life was like during Trochenbrod's darkening last days.

In October 1939, Trochenbrod once again came under Soviet rule. But this time, a well-organized group of Communists in Trochenbrod welcomed Soviet officials. Trochenbrod Communists had been hiding during Polish rule since World War I. Now they could come into the open and were joined by Communist comrades, both Jewish and gentile, freed by the Soviets from Polish prisons. The transition to Communist ways started immediately.

The Soviets installed local Jewish Communists in official positions. They closed the post office. They took over the small factories, workshops, even some of the town's small stores. They made the owners and workers equal and put the workers in charge as a group. Most family businesses without workers were allowed to continue, but some were taken over by upper-level Communists "on behalf of the people." Trochenbrod was being driven into poverty. Food was rationed through a cooperative store. People hid their property, including food they had stored, and relied on the black market for basic goods. It became steadily more difficult for

Trochenbroders to earn money, and at the same time, there was less and less available to buy.

The Soviets were not particularly anti-Jewish, and when they took over the public school, they allowed classes for Trochenbrod pupils to be conducted in Yiddish, though of course all students also had to study the Russian language. In accordance with Communist ideology, the Soviets strongly discouraged religion—they interfered with synagogue prayers and tried to force Trochenbroders to work on the Sabbath. But in the end, because on a day-to-day basis everything was run mostly by local people, ways could often be found to get around the new Communist regulations. Tuvia Drori, who had been a member of the Beitar Zionist Youth group, spoke to me about life at that time; he also wrote about that period in his book, *Ani Ma'amin*:

> Everybody knew everybody in our small town of Trochenbrod. Together we played, and as we grew up, we talked and argued. We Beitar people knew the secrets of the Communists who were hiding—sometimes we even helped them against the Polish police—and they were aware of our Etzel courses held in town. They knew we had weapons and used live ammunition during the drills because they heard the gunshots.
>
> When the Soviets arrived in October 1939, at first they tried to pull us into Communist activity and convince us to become Communists, which would also be good for work and social purposes; they tried to draw us to their assemblies, social activities, and theatrical shows, but we would not do it.

Then they decided to arrest us, probably because of pressures from higher-ups. In my case it was one of my former pupils who came to arrest me. In the first interrogation we were asked about the weapons we had and whether the Beitar youth organization was still active. We didn't take those interrogations too seriously. The social closeness among us was too strong for them to do us any harm.

Eventually we were released and allowed to go home, but it was obvious we could not sit idly waiting for the next arrest. The hopes that maybe the war would cease and we would be able to continue our Zionist activities diminished. Contacts with the outside world were cut off completely, and we could not bear staying citizens under Stalin's[24] regime.

At the end of autumn, a group of us from Beitar decided to start moving out, to find a way to Eretz Yisrael. We knew we would have to steal borders. We didn't know where we would end up, as we would be going only on uncharted routes.

TUVIA DRORI, LUTSK, 1992.
*Photographer unknown; photograph provided by Tuvia Drori.*

24. Stalin was the leader of the Soviet Union at that time.

Soon after the Soviet Union took control, between 20 and 30 Trochenbrod young people, like Tuvia and his Beitar friends, sneaked away in groups of 4 and 5, one after the other, intending to find a way to get to Palestine, which the Zionist groups called Eretz Yisrael, the Land of Israel. They usually left at night and suffered tearful separations from their families; but some slipped out without a face-to-face goodbye because their parents did not want them to leave. None of them ever saw their families again.

YOUNG EAST EUROPEAN JEWS ON THEIR WAY TO PALESTINE
AT THE "INTERNAT," VILNA, SPRING 1940.
*Photographer unknown: photograph provided by Hana Tzipporen.*

Most made their way to Vilna (Vilnius). Vilna was often referred to as the Jerusalem of Lithuania. Its 100,000 Jews accounted for 45% of its population. Vilna was perhaps the most important center of Judaism and Jewish scholarship in what had been the Jewish Pale of Settlement during the rule of the czars in Russia. In Vilna,

Jewish organizations established a shelter called the "Internat" for young people who were fleeing to Palestine from all over Eastern Europe. From Vilna, there were many routes by which these young people made their ways to Palestine, traveling through Turkey, the Soviet Union, Kazakhstan, Uzbekistan, Afghanistan, Iran, Iraq, Syria, Egypt, and Transjordan. Travel through Europe was no longer safe. It took most of them one or two years to make the trip; it took some much longer. Many fell out of contact during their journeys and were never heard from again. A few got stuck along the way in Moscow and ended up fading into Soviet society. Hana Tziporen was 18 years old when she left Trochenbrod in 1939. Here is the story she told me when I interviewed her:

> I was in Beitar, and there was a leader there named Anshel Shpielman. When the war broke out and the Soviets came in, we knew there was no way but to try to escape to Eretz Yisrael. We heard if we could find a way to get to Vilna in Lithuania, it might be possible to go from there to Palestine.
>
> I went with a friend of mine, Machli Schuster. In Vilna, at the Internat, we slept together in one bed. There was only one toilet for everyone, one shower for everyone. We had a communal kitchen. There were Jews in Vilna who gave work to refugees like us so we could earn some money.
>
> At the Internat, there were several people from Trochenbrod, and many others, trying to get to Palestine. . . . We wanted to get to Moscow because we heard it was possible to go onward from

HANA TZIPOREN AT THE GROUNDBREAKING FOR THE BET TAL BUILDING, GIVATAYIM, ISRAEL, 1952.
*Photographer unknown; photograph provided by Hana Tziporen.*

there to Palestine.... We needed money for the journey and the visas. Someone was sent to Lutsk, and somehow got the $100 from our parents to get us to Moscow and then maybe a little bit farther.

In Moscow, people went to the Turkish consulate to request transit permits to Palestine.... We wandered around Moscow not knowing what to do. A Jew there recommended that we go to the Persian embassy. So I went, together with people from all political parties, not just Beitar. I received a false entry permit for Iran, and about thirty of us got to Iran.

We stayed in Teheran several months. Then we were told we had to leave Teheran, so we went to the city of Meshet. There we waited and questioned: What will become of us? How will we get to Eretz Yisrael? At that time, Iran was at war with Iraq, so Iraq wouldn't let us pass. We went through the desert by train and made our way to Suez. While on the train, we learned that the Soviet-German war had broken out—the Germans had invaded Eastern Poland where Trochenbrod was. It had been in Soviet hands until then.[25]

We went through the Suez Canal by cargo boat and arrived at Haifa. There the British arrested us. We were in jail for a couple of months, and then the British freed us; they couldn't send us back to anywhere. And that's how we arrived in Eretz Yisrael.

Shmulik Potash left Trochenbrod in 1939 to work at a training farm near Lodz, Poland, run by the General Zionist organization. Jewish youngsters went to this place from everywhere in Eastern Europe to learn skills that would prepare them to live in a Jewish farming settlement in Palestine. When Germany invaded Poland, Shmulik decided to return to Trochenbrod. The easiest way, he thought, was to go to Warsaw first, and then to Trochenbrod. In Trochenbrod, he planned to say goodbye to family and friends, and then make his way to Palestine.

A couple of days after Shmulik arrived in Warsaw, the city was surrounded by the German Army. The Germans shelled and bombed the city for three weeks and destroyed about a third of

---

25. In June 1941, Germany disregarded the Molotov–Ribbentrop Pact and invaded the Soviet Union.

it. Shmulik was stuck there. He didn't know anyone in Warsaw. He wandered around amid the devastation and by some miracle survived. Then, as he tells it, on the eve of the Jewish holiday of Sukkot, the Germans conquered Warsaw. Huge numbers of German troops had been waiting at the edge of the city to swarm in and occupy it.

Shmulik found himself in a rural suburb of Warsaw, trying to figure out what to do. He had nothing to eat. At one point, he dug in an old tomato field looking for scraps. A German soldier came up to him, and Shmulik spoke to the soldier in Yiddish, which was close enough to German to enable them to communicate. The soldier, a young man about 19 years old, challenged Shmulik.

"What are you doing here?"

When he heard Shmulik's story, the soldier made a sausage sandwich from food he had in his knapsack and gave it to Shmulik. The soldier warned Shmulik to go away because there were mines in the tomato field.

The next day, the Germans opened the concertina wire they had strung around the city, and as German soldiers flooded in, people fleeing eastward were able to slip out. Among those who slipped out was Shmulik.

First he traveled to the east—Trochenbrod was about 220 miles southeast from Warsaw. He walked and hitched rides in passing horse-drawn wagons. Shmulik described with wonderment his second positive experience with a German soldier:

I was walking along a road, and a horse-drawn wagon came by with two German soldiers, one driving it. I raised my hand. They came up to me, and the driver said, "Sure, hop on." The two soldiers were talking—I couldn't hear what they said because of the noise of the wheels. Suddenly, the one who was not driving turned and looked at me and jerked his head toward the side of the road in a signal that I should jump off the wagon; the one who held the reins to the horses didn't see the gesture. I understood his signal and jumped. The driver was probably talking about robbing or beating me. A second German soldier had helped me to survive.

Under its pact with Germany, the Soviet Union had occupied what was then Eastern Poland, while Germany occupied Western Poland. They each guarded the border between them carefully because the Soviets didn't trust the Germans, and the Germans didn't trust the Soviets. They each expected the other side to violate the pact. After a number of failed attempts to sneak across the border over several days, one night Shmulik decided to run as fast as he could and hope he wouldn't get caught. When he saw an opening between the guards, he ran like his life depended on it—in fact, his life did depend on it—and to his own surprise, he found himself safely on the Soviet side of the border.

A few days later, Shmulik was back in Trochenbrod, where Trochenbroders greeted him with a joyous celebration. But he found Soviet and Trochenbrod Communists in charge of the town, and Shmulik felt he could not live with that.

Word soon reached Trochenbrod about the way station in Vilna set up to help young pioneers on their way to Palestine. Shmulik made his way to the Internat. From Vilna, he went to Moscow. After Moscow, Shmulik's quest for a way to Palestine took many twists and turns that landed him in one strange place after another—places like the city of Tashkent in Uzbekistan. Finally, 10 years later, in 1949, Shmulik arrived in Palestine. By then, the part of it under Jewish control had become the State of Israel.

SHMULIK POTASH IN AN IMMIGRANT CAMP, ISRAEL, 1950.
*Photographer unknown; photograph provided by Shmulik Potash.*

During this period of Soviet control, not only was there growing poverty because many businesses were not allowed to operate normally, but there was also pressure on adults to join the Communist Party and youngsters to join Communist youth organizations and abandon Judaism. People knew they were watched constantly and could be reported for saying the wrong thing. Food could only be sold and bought legally through a cooperative store run by the Communists. The Communist leaders decided upon the prices paid to Trochenbroders for their produce and the prices people would pay to buy food. Regional trading markets were shut down.

But the people of Trochenbrod could still move around relatively freely, and they were able to maintain their way of life to some degree. Meanwhile, many Jews from Western Poland fled from the Nazis into what had been Eastern Poland, now occupied by the Soviet Union. About 1,000 of them found their way to Trochenbrod and Lozisht.

―――

Nahum Kohn was born and raised in Western Poland; he had been trained as a watchmaker. Soon after the Germans invaded the area where he lived, he fled eastward and found himself in Lutsk. In Lutsk, he eventually found his brother, who had also fled from Western Poland. Much later, after the war, Nahum wrote a book called, *A Voice from the Forest: Memoirs of a Jewish Partisan*, in which he gives us a good sense of what it was like in and around Trochenbrod at that time.

Nahum found work for several months with another watchmaker who had a small business in Lutsk. Under Soviet Communist rules, a person could work on his own but could not have people working

NAHUM KOHN, CANADA, 1970s.
*Photograph provided by Howard Roiter.*

for him. By early 1940, the Soviets began to enforce their idea of Communist socialism, and Nahum was required to work for a state-run collective workshop for watchmakers. Like the cooperative store in Trochenbrod, this "collective" watchmaker workshop was really just a state-run business in which Communist leaders decided how much the workers would be paid to repair watches and how much customers would have to pay to have their watches repaired.

One day, after many months, Soviet officials rounded up the refugees from Western Poland in Lutsk and sent them on trains to labor camps in Siberia. Nahum thought they did this because the Soviets didn't trust the Germans, and they suspected there were spies for Germany among the refugees. Not long after the train started moving, Nahum and his brother jumped off. They hid in the forest for a few days, and then walked back to Lutsk.

They found their way to a large stable in Lutsk. The stable was owned by a Jew, who let them hide there among the horses. But they needed to work and earn money. After a week of hiding, Nahum took a chance and went to the local Soviet government office and asked how he could find work. After looking at Nahum's documents, the official knew Nahum was not supposed to be there, but he was a kind man. He pretended the documents were fine and told Nahum he was not allowed to work in Lutsk but could find work in a small lumbering town 25 miles to the east. Nahum and his brother understood the official was signaling to Nahum that it was dangerous for him to stay in Lutsk.

The stable owner told them about "two villages of Jewish peasants" not far from Lutsk. Schuster, a friend of his from Trochenbrod, would visit him soon, and he would ask if "something can be arranged." In a couple of weeks, Nahum and his brother looked wide-eyed down the street of a now much poorer Trochenbrod. In his book, Nahum wrote:

> When we arrived there, it was the first time in my life that I saw Jewish farmers. I could never have imagined this, and I rejoiced when I saw them. Everyone had primitive leather-working equipment at home, and they worked on hides. So they lived from their fields, their cows, their horses, and their hides. They were totally surrounded by forests; the nearest road was 20 or 30 kilometers

away. I was curious, so I used to ask old-timers how they came to be there. They told me that the area had been totally unsettled and wild when their ancestors came. . . .

With our watch-repairing skills, we could earn something. The people in Trochenbrod didn't have wristwatches, but they had ancient clocks on their walls. Before our arrival there had been no watchmaker. So they brought these antiques to us and bartered food in exchange for repairs. . . .

## German Rule

A few months after Nahum arrived in Trochenbrod, the German Army invaded Soviet-occupied territory to their east and took control of Trochenbrod. The National Socialist, or Nazi party, was in control of Germany and completely controlled the German Army. Many people called the German Army in World War II the Nazi Army.

Nahum had run away from the Nazis when they had invaded Western Poland because he saw the terrible things they did to Jews. When the Nazis took over Trochenbrod, it was clear to Nahum that he had to get away and fight them somehow. He gathered a small group of men, mostly young Trochenbroders, and they went into the forest. They learned to live there, and they taught themselves to fight. Soldiers in units like these who fought from the forest and were not part of an actual army in World War II were called "partisans." They attacked German army units venturing into the forest. They attacked German supply trains. They attacked Ukrainians who told the Nazis about their Jewish neighbors in hiding. They attacked Ukrainians who had tortured and killed Jews. This little partisan unit Nahum had created was eventually destroyed by the Nazis, who of course had bigger and better weapons and many more men. Nahum and two others from the unit survived the Nazi attacks, and in the end, survived the war.

---

Trochenbrod and Lozisht had a combined population of more than 6,000 people, Jewish people, when the Germans invaded lands occupied by the Soviet Union on June 22, 1941. About 1,000 were refugees from Western Poland. In the first days after their invasion of Trochenbrod, the Germans began to show their cruelty toward Jews. They marked the town's houses with six-pointed "Jewish stars" as a way of announcing that a type of people worth much less than other people lived there. They shot anyone who did not immediately do as the Nazis ordered them to do or who were suspected of violating the new anti-Jewish regulations.

The Germans let their Ukrainian helpers know it was acceptable for them to take anything from houses with Jewish stars on them or to destroy Jewish property. The Germans also set up Ukrainian police units to control the Jews, hunt them down when they tried to escape the terror in Trochenbrod, and assist the Nazis in their mass killing "aktions." People who had been friendly with Trochenbroders before, people from nearby villages, suddenly turned up as Nazi collaborators

*The* LOST TOWN

and treated their Jewish neighbors with cruelty and brutality.

The Germans set up a local Judenrat (pronounced **Yewd**enrat), or Jewish Council, which had to carry out some of their cruel anti-Jewish rules—the Judenrat had to collect "taxes" and provide Jews as forced labor for the Germans. Like other villages and towns, Trochenbrod had to supply a quota of slave workers for the German Army. Most of them were sent to the railroad depot in Kivertzy 14 miles away on unpaved roads. The Judenrat had to meet the quota, but the Ukrainian police would also snatch people off the street for these work crews. Each work crew labored a week, loading and unloading trains or hauling building supplies, before it was replaced by a new crew of fresh workers. The workers slept on the floors in empty warehouses and stables near the railroad station. At night, the men in these crews were beaten and terrorized by their Ukrainian guards and German overseers. Some men never returned to Trochenbrod.

In October, the Germans confiscated all the farmland in Trochenbrod, then took away all the livestock. Next, they took the townspeople's furs, other warm clothing, and valuable property like farm equipment. They commanded Jews to pay heavy special taxes. Meanwhile, Ukrainian collaborators stole gold, silver, and other valuables from Jews, threatening them with death if they did not turn over their property. Trochenbrod Jews were left with no way to support themselves.

Jews were not allowed to leave Trochenbrod, work the farm

fields, or trade with people outside the town. Again, a black market flourished: milk, grain, flour, potatoes, and fat were smuggled into Trochenbrod in exchange for clothing, valuables, or money. The trade was carried on at night. Being caught meant immediate death. Blacksmiths, shoemakers, and other individual craftsmen were still able to make a meager living from their work, but many Trochenbroders began to starve, trying to stay alive on rotten food and scraps from German and Ukrainian trash bins.

Jewish life in Trochenbrod became worthless. Within a few months of the start of German control, the recently proud and thriving town of Trochenbrod was reduced to poverty, hunger, terror, slavery, beatings, humiliation, and misery of every kind. Over the wretchedness of Trochenbroders hung the possibility of death falling on anyone anywhere at any time for any reason or for no reason. This was the life of Trochenbrod's Jews, of the people of Trochenbrod, until the end of their days.

As winter turned into spring in 1942, it became clear to many Trochenbrod townspeople that the Germans planned eventually to kill them all—by slave labor, starvation, or with guns. Some Trochenbrod families built false walls in their houses or farm buildings. This created a narrow space between the false and true walls in which they could hide if the Nazis started rounding up people. Some dug shallow pits in the forest and covered them with branches and leaves to hide them; they would try to live in these bunkers if they could escape to the forest when the time came. Some managed to obtain false identity papers and slipped away from Trochenbrod at night. And some young men, like Nahum Kohn, fled into the forest and trained themselves to be partisans.

Most Trochenbroders, however, could not imagine an escape or what they could do to save themselves and their families. They struggled to survive, they became more and more miserable and desperate, and they awaited their fate.

---

I was struck by the stories of what took place in Trochenbrod under Nazi rule. Some Ukrainian people who had been friends of Trochenbrod Jews suddenly began acting like cruel barbarians, beating and killing their old friends and plundering their houses. But in contrast, a few Ukrainian and Polish families took great risks to themselves and their families to hide and feed their Jewish neighbors. Sometimes, it was a deliberate action, like bringing food to a Jewish family hiding in the forest; sometimes, it was a deliberate non-action, like not reporting seeing a Jew looking for food in a farm field. Sometimes, it was both.

A Ukrainian in the nearby village of Yaromel, for example, told me that his father hid "a very good person named Itzik, from Trochenbrod" in their house for a few days. Then, the Germans began searching all the houses very carefully looking for Jews, and death was the punishment for anyone caught hiding a Jew; so they had no choice but "to say goodbye" to Itzik.

One Trochenbrod survivor told me about a Polish family that hid her family. Later, when they had to hide in a bunker in the forest, the Polish family brought food to them. Another told me of Ukrainians who let Jews hiding in the forest come and warm themselves in their houses in the winter; they would also feed them and give them food from their gardens. An elderly Ukrainian woman, living in a village close to Trochenbrod, told me about a family friend, a red-haired Trochenbroder. He obtained a false passport that identified him as Ukrainian and sneaked away from Trochenbrod at night. He stopped at their house to say goodbye, hid with them for a day, and then continued walking to Lutsk to get lost among the crowds. People in the nearby Ukrainian village of Klubochin helped Trochenbrod families survive in the forest and helped young Trochenbrod men who formed partisan groups.

The Nazis planned for Ukraine to be mostly "Judenrein," free of Jews, by October 10, 1942. According to their plan, most of the Jews of each town and village were to be murdered on a designated day, and then the remainder in one or two additional "aktions" they would carry out later. August 11, 1942, was the day on which the Nazis scheduled the slaughter of most of Trochenbrod's Jews. They adhered to their schedule.

## Darkness

In the early morning hours of Sunday, August 9, 1942, 20 men of Einsatzgruppe C, one of the German killing units, rode into

Trochenbrod on motorcycles. Following the motorcycles were 11 German Army trucks, carrying about 100 Ukrainian police troops, called Shutsmen, who served the Nazis. The Shutsmen spread out and ordered all the Jews of Trochenbrod and Lozisht to go immediately to the center of Trochenbrod for a meeting. At the meeting the Germans would issue special cards allowing the townspeople to work and earn some money. This was a trick to get Trochenbrod's Jews to go to the center of town and not try to run away.

After a long wait, the German commander arrived. He announced he had established a ghetto—a confined area where Jews must live—in Trochenbrod. He told 50 leather workers to move with their families into a group of houses at the north end of town, where they would continue making and repairing leather goods for German soldiers. People were allowed to return to their homes to gather clothing and other small items for their stay in the ghetto but had to be back within two hours.

The Shutsmen lined up along the sides of the street and screamed, "Hurry up!" at the people carrying sacks of belongings on their way back to the newly created ghetto. They shot anyone they found trying to hide or escape. They looked in the houses, and anyone they found lingering, not rushing to collect a few possessions and run back to the ghetto, they dragged outside and shot.

But some Trochenbroders understood that the return to the ghetto might be the last walk of their lives. They dropped their sacks and raced to the forest, running in the drainage canals alongside the farm fields for cover whenever they could. Many were shot as they tried to escape this way.

The next day, August 10, 1942, was quiet. There was no life in Trochenbrod except in the ghettos and in the barracks of Germans and Shutsmen. People who had managed to escape to the forest saw Germans and Shutsmen searching for them and killing anyone they found. Some decided their situation in the forest was hopeless, so they sneaked back into the ghetto at night to share their fate with their fellow Trochenbroders. Many still believed, or convinced themselves, they would be assigned to forced labor crews and nothing more.

The following day, August 11, 1942, Trochenbrod's Jews were told to prepare for transport: they should bring food for three days with them. They were piled into trucks and taken, group after group, to pits in the Yaromel Forest about two miles away. There, they were ordered to climb into the pits and were shot.

Late in the afternoon, the Nazis completed their first "aktion," their first mass murder action, in Trochenbrod. On that day, more than 4,500 people from Trochenbrod and Lozisht were killed at the Yaromel mass grave pits. The trucks made a final trip back to Trochenbrod carrying the clothing and other things taken from the murdered townspeople for storage in empty Trochenbrod houses.

Somehow, between 500 and 1000 people remained alive in Trochenbrod's ghetto, and the slave laborers, primarily leather workers, also remained in their separate small ghetto. Over the next few weeks, the remaining Jews left in the ghetto were joined by a steady flow of others who had escaped into the forest, but now decided they had no choice but to return. Yom Kippur, the Day of Atonement, fell on September 21. As that day grew closer, more and more people came in from the forest to spend what they knew was likely to be their last Yom Kippur, praying with their Trochenbrod friends and relatives. Nazis surrounded the ghetto houses, took everyone to the pits, and murdered them the same way the first group had been murdered nearly six weeks earlier. The remaining leather workers were murdered a few months later. The people of Trochenbrod were gone.

The Germans dismantled many houses and shipped the lumber back to Germany. The buildings that remained were soon destroyed by partisans so they could not be used by Germans or Ukrainians. People from surrounding villages took what was left. Even the paving stones were carried off from the small section of Trochenbrod's street where the paving project had been started. Now both the people and the buildings were gone. Trochenbrod had vanished.

CHAPTER FIVE

# Darkness: Khaim Fights

Of the more than 6,000 people in Trochenbrod and Lozisht when the Nazis invaded, about 33 escaped during the mass murders and survived. These were people who fled across the front lines to the Soviet Union; or obtained false documents and made themselves "disappear"; or hid with Polish or Ukrainian families; or became partisans before the Nazis could trap them and did not die in battle; or fled into the forest and somehow survived there. Several hundred at first found ways to escape Nazi brutality and murder, but most of them did not survive the war: they were discovered and murdered, killed fighting the Nazis as Soviet soldiers or partisans, or perished in hiding.

Three survivors of those last awful days shared their voices and stories with me: Khaim Votchin, Basia-Ruchel Potash, and Ryszard

Lubinski. When you read Khaim, Basia-Ruchel, and Ryszard's stories, remember that the Nazis murdered Jews and terrified everyone else—non-Jews knew they would be shot immediately if they were found helping or hiding Jews. And so, every act of kindness toward Jews, every act of revenge against the Nazi murderers, every struggle to survive, every help given so that someone might live—all these were acts of great risk and heroism.

KHAIM VOTCHIN AS A SOLDIER IN A RED ARMY UNIFORM, 1944.
*Photograph provided by Khaim Votchin, from a Red Army field newspaper.*

Khaim agreed to meet me in 2008 in his modest apartment in Haifa, Israel, to tell me about his experiences as a Trochenbrod partisan. He was born in a village about 50 miles from Trochenbrod-Lozisht. His father died when he was very young, and with his mother and her second husband, Khaim moved to Lozisht when he was six years old. He was athletic and strong-willed and did not follow traditional paths. He was very good with mathematics and languages and from a young age used these talents to earn a living as a teacher.

He had the right set of skills and interests to be a partisan leader.

One day in 1942, a German soldier ordered Khaim to catch one of his chickens for the soldier's dinner, and then as Khaim described it, "The soldier stood there with his chest pushed out and his thumbs in his belt exploding in laughter" as Khaim chased after the chicken in his yard. This humiliation convinced Khaim that Germans were cruel, he could not live around them, and he had to fight them. He told me he knew nothing about fighting or guns or living in the forest, but began making plans. And then, he said:

> Others came to me, and we discussed how we could be partisans: where we could get weapons; how we could live in the forest; how we could learn to be fighters; how we could get started without the Germans or Ukrainians finding out; and so on.
>
> We formed a committee and handed out jobs: acquire weapons; convince Trochenbrod young men to join us; make a plan to move Trochenbrod people to the forest; figure out the best way to get food in the forest; and try to contact the Ukrainian Communists, who already had partisan units operating in the area. It was important to find the Ukrainian Communists because they were probably in contact with the Red Army of the Soviet Union and could get supplies from them. Also, we heard that a leader of Ukrainian Communists operated in the Radziwill Forest, and maybe he could tell us how to get weapons.
>
> Alexander Felyuk, the partisan leader, was from the village of Klubochin a few kilometers through the forest east of Trochenbrod.

We talked to his mother, and then met him in the Radziwill Forest. Prince Janush Radziwill had stationed armed rangers in his forest to protect his property. Felyuk said, "If you're brave, let's go take the guns from those forest rangers."

Alexander Felyuk worked with us for several months and made us into partisans. He was a wonderful man. He died recently, but we stayed in touch with him all these years. We sent him money and packages.

One day, one of our boys found a new pistol with bullets in the Ignatovka Cemetery. It had been left behind when the Soviet soldiers ran away. With this pistol, we learned how to use guns and went to a forest ranger, waited until he had to come down from his tower, and then took his rifle.

With one rifle, we went into the forest and armed ourselves. We took more rifles from rangers, and then stole more rifles and also ammunition and grenades from German Army warehouses. Eventually, we had 30 people in our group of armed partisans, and I was the commander.

And so we began to operate. A Jew came to us and said that a certain Ukrainian found a Jew and turned him over to the Germans. This Ukrainian was called Gapon. Immediately four of us went to Gapon's village. We took him to the forest and shot him.

After that, we heard that the Germans arranged to send the animals left behind in Trochenbrod to Germany. We found the herd, ready for transfer to the train station, and we went in and set them free and scattered them all.

A very terrible Shutsman who had done horrible things to Jews lived in a small village called Yaromel near Trochenbrod. This was a Ukrainian village with mostly straw-roofed houses. For our third operation, we went to his house and pounded on his window: "We are Shutsmen. We have an important message for you. Glory to Ukraine. Open up." The man came and we drank with him. He bragged about all the Jews he had killed—this included women and children—and others he had turned over to the Nazis. Then we showed him who we were. His wife screamed, and we took him away in a horse wagon driven by a hired Polish man. We took him to the forest and shot him. The Polish man was happy to be a part of the operation. He was a good man and he had a good time. Revenge felt sweet, revenge for the blood of all the children, women, and men the Shutsman had murdered.

That's how we started. We didn't know anything about how to fight battles yet, so we started with small operations like this.

The Nazis were able to fool many people. Many of Trochenbrod's Jews believed the Germans would not kill them even though they saw death in front of them. Once we planned to attack Trochenbrod and kill the Germans and Shutsmen there. We would throw grenades into the houses where the Germans and Shutsmen lived, then open fire and kill anybody left. Another group would set fires in different places, burning anything the Germans wanted to have. We sent word to the Jews in the ghetto, warning them to sneak away to the forest. Soon, one of the Jews from the ghetto showed up and said he was sent to beg us to do nothing. The Jews would not leave. They believed the German promises of no more killings, so they did not want to leave Trochenbrod. We begged them, but they would not listen. Those Jews saved the lives of the Germans and Shutsmen. Soon they were murdered by them.

Some Trochenbrod Jews escaped to the forest and stayed there. They did their best in a difficult situation, but they suffered. They dug their shelters into the ground in hidden parts of the forest. They camouflaged their shelters with loose dirt, tree limbs, and leaves. They built some shelters in the swamps. We helped the families as much as we could. After every raid, we brought them food, clothing, and boots. Also, we instructed them on how to live better in the forest. That's how far we had come in a month or two—now we taught others how to survive in the forest!

---

In October 1942, one of our partisans, Yosef, came back from a forest nearby after he visited Jews hiding there. On the way to our camp, he stumbled on a band of Soviet paratroopers who had parachuted in to blow up Nazi trains. They hid in the bushes, and he actually almost tripped on them. Imagine the tension there was until they figured out that they could talk together. Yosef told them he would bring the leaders of his partisan unit who were only a kilometer or two away. We went to meet them.

Their two leaders came toward us. One was a short older man, about 40 years old. The other one had light hair and was about

25 years old. They had red stars on their hats and brand new shiny automatic rifles. With just a few steps between us, we stopped and stared at each other. When we started to talk, the older man took out a cigarette pack from his pocket and offered us a smoke. They explained they were Soviet military explosives experts sent to blow up German trains.

I told them, "We are a small group, but we are well-organized and we'll be honored to help you destroy the Fascists."[26] We told them about our activities, hopes, and our men. They taught a few of us how to blow up trains and took us on operations to do that. They agreed to fight together with us when we attacked the Nazis and Shutsmen in Trochenbrod.

---

Fall had started. The storks were migrating, and many other birds flew above us to their winter places. The paratroopers and our men successfully blew up the railroad. They derailed trains almost every night. How things had changed! Just a short time ago, the Germans were like gods, and now every night they were terrified, at least on the trains.

Then the Germans made local villagers help guard the tracks. Each guard had a piece of track he walked up and down and a whistle to blow in case they saw something suspicious. A German detachment stood in the train station, ready to move if there was an alert. This made our jobs more difficult but not impossible. We

---

26. Fascists is another name for Nazis and other dictatorial political parties, especially during World War II.

crawled toward the rails, waited for the guard to walk in the other direction, then crawled the last 100 or 200 meters, put the explosives where it should go, and crawled away. When a train passed over, we exploded the charge by wire from a distance.

Alexander Felyuk went away to make contact with a group of partisans we had heard about located much farther north. On his way back to us, he stopped at his village, Klubochin, where his mother and family lived. He learned the Germans had entered the village and rounded up a large group of men, women, and children. They took them to a pit in the forest and murdered them all, including Alex's mother, brother, and little daughter. This was Nazi "payment" for 20 people from Klubochin, including Alex, who were partisans. The other 19 partisans were in Klubochin when the Germans came, so they were murdered.

In November, we had a big battle with German soldiers. We fought them off. Now, we fought German detachments and won! The Germans were surprised there was an organized group with weapons, and we knew they decided they had to wipe us out. They would come again soon, and this time they would probably bring Ukrainian Shutsmen to fight with them against us. What could we do? Should we stay and try to outsmart them? It had begun to snow, which meant when we went from one of our shelters or storage caves to another one, we left a trail and "asked" for an attack. We also had a problem that we didn't have enough ammunition. We saw that we couldn't keep going like this, so we left the Trochenbrod area.

Alex said we should go to the Pripyat swamps in the north, in Byelorussia.[27] Because of what he learned on his travels, he was sure we would find large partisan camps which we could join. They received Soviet support and weapons. Our Soviet paratroopers wanted to stay and continue their work blowing up Nazi trains. Although it was Alex's idea to go north, he decided to stay in the Klubochin area. He joined Medvedev's partisan detachment. This Soviet detachment was based at Lopaten, not far from Klubochin and Trochenbrod. Their main activity was to sabotage German operations and assassinate high-level German officers in Rovno, which the Germans used as their central administration center.

A BUNKER IN MEDVEDEV'S PARTISAN CAMP, LOPATEN, AS IT APPEARS TODAY.
*Photograph by the author.*

As we moved north, we found village after village and town after town where the Jews had been murdered and their possessions stolen or destroyed. Although I had taught Jewish studies, in my

---

27. Byelorussia means White Russia and refers to a country called Belarus today.

heart I was not really a very religious man. And when I saw what happened to the people in Trochenbrod and all the other villages and towns, I knew that never in my life again could I even think about a god who saw and heard all this but just sat there watching.

In Byelorussia, we found scouts from a Soviet partisan group, and they took us to the base camp of a large partisan detachment. We agreed to become part of this detachment, and that night, in December 1942, our Jewish partisan group, Trochenbrod's partisan unit, no longer existed.

Months later, a decision from the High Command arrived telling us we should move south to the Carpathian Mountains to conduct certain operations there. On the way, we passed through the Radziwill Forest. The Jews in Trochenbrod and Lozisht had all been murdered by then. We made up a unit of 400 raiders to hunt down the Ukrainians who had helped the Nazis in their murder. We killed many of them and burned their houses.

We decided to burn everything we could that was left in Trochenbrod because we didn't want the Nazis or the Ukrainians to use any of the houses or to benefit from any of the buildings. Jews had owned the flour mill but after they killed the Jews, Ukrainians took it over. We didn't want them to have the flour mill, so we burned it. We gathered straw, spread it around, and spilled fuel that had been used to run the machinery on everything. Then we lit the fire and burned down the flour mill. Although sad, the feeling of revenge was very strong and very satisfying.

CHAPTER SIX
# Darkness: Basia-Ruchel Survives

Basia-Ruchel Potash, age 6, 1936.
*Studio photograph made in Lutsk; photograph provided by Betty Gold.*

The second survivor I interviewed was Eli Potash's daughter, Basia-Ruchel Potash, born in 1930. When I first met her after my initial trip to Trochenbrod, she had been living in America for more than 50 years and went by the name of Betty Gold. I called Betty when I returned from that first trip because a cousin of hers living in the city of Lutsk asked me to call to convey the cousin's greetings. Betty and I had been good friends ever since that first phone call. She lived in Beechwood, a suburb of Cleveland. I visited and interviewed her many times to piece together the full remarkable story of how she and her family survived the Holocaust.

Betty spoke of a delightful childhood in Trochenbrod before the war, surrounded by a warm extended family, lots of friends, wonderful experiences, the freedoms of a rural life, and a strong sense of community. It all ended when the Soviets and then the Germans occupied Trochenbrod. At age 12, Betty went into hiding with her family in the Radziwill Forest. She and her family suffered greatly, but when the fighting ended, Betty and her family had triumphed.

> My father and his cousin had a big wooden shed behind our house. It was long and narrow. They would store wood and tools and other things in there. Because of what they heard from refugees from Western Poland, they decided—just in case—to build a false wall in the shed, so that if the Nazis came to get us, we could go behind the false wall and hide. They built it secretly at night.
>
> Later—I remember it was a hot summer day—the Germans and Ukrainians surrounded Trochenbrod, and they took everybody out of their homes. We all had to schlep whatever we could carry and go to certain houses in the middle of town. This was the Trochenbrod ghetto. I was with my immediate family—my father, mother, two brothers, and my grandmother, who lived with us at the time.

My other grandmother lived across the street and hid since she didn't want to go to the ghetto. Before we left, we saw she had been found and shot.

Once we got to the ghetto, my family and my father's cousin's family went back to the house because we were allowed to go back to get some things if we returned to the ghetto within two hours. I was left in the ghetto with my grandmother to watch our belongings. I sat with her, and I saw that nobody came back from my family. Right away, I thought they must be hiding behind the false wall. And I got scared, and I got angry. Why had they left me? And I was torn. My grandmother sat with our belongings, and I sat next to her, and all the other Jews were there. I didn't know what to do. I wanted to live. I wanted to go back to find my family. She couldn't go back. So I left her. That was a very tough day in my life.

I ran to our house at the south end of town. As I ran down the street, all the people walked toward the ghetto while I ran the other way. And there were the Nazis and Ukrainians with their guns. One of the Germans was busy looking up at something, so I crawled right between his legs. As I got close to my house, I saw there were soldiers in the distance, so I crawled on the ground between the twigs and the bushes along the side of my house.

I got to our house and went to the shed and found my family, including my uncles and cousins, behind the false wall. There were 17 of us in the hiding space behind the false wall, including three small children. We weren't allowed to cough, or even breathe loudly, because Nazis were all around. We held our mouths; the grownups stuffed rags and things in our mouths so we wouldn't sneeze or cough or talk.

Vertical boards created the false wall. I looked through a crack between the boards and saw two German soldiers. They led people to the ghetto, but they grabbed babies and threw them into a truck. The mothers reached for their babies and screamed. There was nothing we could have done; if I had gone out they would have thrown me in the truck, too.

I thought, Maybe they'll just take them to the ghetto. They don't want them to walk because they don't have patience to wait until babies and toddlers and little kids will get there.

No. Nothing like that.

A day passed. From behind the false wall, we heard a lot of shooting. I did not see what happened, but we heard the shooting clearly, maybe a mile or two away. We found out from a survivor who ran away from the shooting that they had taken the rabbi, the parents, and the children to a big pit to shoot them. Some ran away, some were shot trying to run away. Some made it to the forest.

We couldn't get out from our hiding place the next day because they had chosen our house to store valuables and clothes they had taken from other houses and from the people they had killed. There were so many soldiers there, unloading and packing and moving things, that we couldn't escape. We had to wait through another night and day. The next night, in the middle of the night, we crawled out into a garden next to the shed where we hid. It rained, and we were grateful for the noise it made. We hoped nobody would hear us. We crawled to the canals that drained the water. They were long, maybe half a mile. In the canals, we crawled to the Radziwill Forest.

After a short while, things seemed to calm down, and we went back to the ghetto. Almost everybody had come back for Yom Kippur. The Germans and Ukrainians surrounded the ghetto, took everyone from their houses, and killed them all.

How did we get out of it? My father threw us out the window and yelled, "Run, and we'll meet you in the forest." Our parents were the last to get out of the window, after the children were thrown out.

Everyone running to the woods through the drainage canals had to run and jump over the bodies of their friends and relatives who had been shot running in the canals—some were dead, some were bleeding, some of them screamed for help.

My father yelled, "Run, run, run, don't stop," and we jumped over dead and dying people we knew, our own flesh and blood, while we ran to save our lives. Can you imagine how your heart aches with guilt and pain because of this?

We were able to hide in the forest at that time because there were still trees with plenty of leaves that hid us. While we stayed there, my father and his cousin and a couple of other men who were with us decided they would build bunkers in different spots in the forest to prepare for the winter. If they found us in one spot, we'd have someplace else to run to. They dug nine bunkers over a few months and covered them with twigs and tree limbs. They would leave a small entrance where someone could crawl in. The roofs of the bunkers looked like the forest floor.

While it was warm, we stayed outside. At one point, my father and the other men decided the safest place to stay was in a nearby marshy area where the trees were thick. They built a platform from tree limbs over the water, and we lived there day and night. To survive, we would go out at night. Mostly, I would go out because my brother was circumcised, and if he was caught they could pull down his pants and see he was Jewish. I had a little babushka,[28] and I would go out and find as much food as I could in the yards and orchards of villagers.

In order for me to get back to the family, I'd clap my hands, since it could have been some forest animal noise. When I clapped, they'd clap back to me, and that's how they directed me to the platform with the food—apples or a piece of bread or whatever I could get. For water, we used rainwater caught in a little pot or sometimes we drank from the swamp. And we just sat there with nothing to do.

At the time, there was a Polish gentile family my father told about our hiding. We were hungry and didn't have anything to eat. He told them because he figured we had nothing to lose—we were finished anyway. The Polish family had been my father's customers and also his friends, so he thought maybe they'd help us. And they did.

When my mother ran away from Trochenbrod, she took with her a few Russian gold coins. We gave these to the Polish

---

28. A babushka is a light decorative scarf worn by Ukrainian women over their hair. Wearing a babushka, Basia-Ruchel looked more like a Ukrainian girl.

family—there wasn't much—and they'd drop off a few packages of food here and there. We were extremely grateful. It was a lifesaver for us, and they did not report us. They were loyal and righteous people.

THE POLISH LUDWIKOWSKI FAMILY THAT HELPED ELI POTASH
AND HIS FAMILY SURVIVE IN THE FOREST, 1948.
*Photographer unknown; photograph provided by Betty Gold.*

After that, winter set in, and we started to hide in the bunkers. We had with us a coat lined with fur. Don't ask me how or why, but my parents, when they ran from the house in the ghetto, took with them my father's fur-lined coat. It was our only protection from the terrible cold, in addition to any clothing we had that didn't fall apart. We treasured it. The winter was disastrous because you couldn't go out for food—your steps would leave a trail right to bunker. If you didn't eat for three days, you just didn't eat for three days. You had to wait to walk in a snowstorm or until the snow melted.

One time, my brother stole seven loaves of bread from a Polish home. What a wonderful thing! When he came back, we almost attacked him. Everybody wanted the bread. My dad dug a little shelf inside the bunker, and he stored the breads there. He gave us a speech that the bread needed to last as long as possible since it was winter. Nobody got more than one piece a day. He showed us the size of the piece for each day with his fingers.

In the bunker, we slept on the ground, of course. My place was next to the shelf. I couldn't help myself: I'd pick little pieces of the bread and suck it like a lollypop. I picked and picked and picked. The next day, my parents said they thought a rat was in the bunker, eating the bread. Finally, I admitted I was the rat, so they made me sleep on the other side. The bread lasted about a month.

There were nine people in the bunker. We would lie side by side, and if one person turned over, everybody had to turn. It was a shallow dugout. We could sit up, but we couldn't stand up. We were lying there day and night, looking at each other, hardly talking. And eventually the coat with the fur lining got full of lice, so we had to get rid of it. The lice got into our hair—I had very long pigtails, and my father and cousin both cut my hair off with their knives.

One time, our Polish friend Yuzef came to warn us the Germans were going to search for a bunker of Jews in the forest that night. We knew about another group from Trochenbrod who had also run away and were in a bunker about two miles away. My father went there to beg them to let us in their bunker because we had to leave ours. There was not any room in their bunker, and they couldn't let us stay. So we remained in our bunker.

My father said we couldn't escape—whatever would happen would happen. He sat us down and said, "Look, when they come here to kill us, here's what we're going to do. Don't wait. Get out and run. You'll get shot, but at least you'll be shot on the run and not be caught and tortured." Then we started kissing each other goodbye. When my father kissed my mother goodbye he said, "Stay well." We laughed. We really giggled when he said that. If not for a sense of humor, I don't think we would have survived because that's the only thing that kept us going. We laughed at ourselves and cried at ourselves because we just ran out of emotions.

We waited. And waited. All of a sudden, we heard shooting—grenades and gunshots. Terrible, terrible sounds. What happened? It was the other bunker, the one we wanted to stay in, that the Germans had discovered, and they killed all the people who hid there. That was our luck. A miracle. Go figure it out. We had been ready to die.

There was now so much snow, we couldn't go out. We stayed there so they wouldn't find us, but we needed food. Yuzef couldn't come either because of the snow. We were hungry and cold. We didn't have clothes, and our feet were wrapped in leaves. I still suffer because my toes were frozen. My mother would hold my feet to her body to try to warm them up. My father would blow through his cupped hands on my hands and feet to warm them.

We thought there was still a ghetto in Trochenbrod, and we decided to go there. Whatever happened to everybody else would happen to us also. We couldn't take it anymore. We started to leave and moved toward Trochenbrod in the night. We could have walked blindfolded, that's how well we knew the forest. But we walked for hours and hours. We couldn't understand how we had lost our way back to Trochenbrod. It wasn't that far; it was only a few miles. Exhausted, confused, and frail from starving, we couldn't walk anymore. We sat in a trench and rested, waiting for the sun to come up. While we sat there, we heard a lot of shooting but we didn't know what it was.

When daylight came, we saw the fields behind Trochenbrod houses. We had been close to Trochenbrod and didn't realize it. The men went to find people. They crawled to a house and climbed in through the window, and there was nobody there. They went to another house, and there was nobody there, either. We found out later that all the people in the ghetto had been killed before, and the shots we heard were the killings of the last leather workers, who had been held in the synagogue. Getting lost had been a second miracle.

I don't know why we didn't commit suicide. Nobody wanted to live anymore. We didn't know what to do. At night, we turned around and went to another bunker. We had nothing to eat, and it had been three days. We were literally starving; our tongues were hanging out. We ate snow. We picked any leaves we could find and ate them. We usually threw up.

There was another bunker not far from us. There was a father, a three-year-old girl, and a few other people, all from Trochenbrod. The little girl became sick and died. They had to leave their bunker because somebody spotted them. And they also spotted us. So we all left our bunkers, and we left the little girl under a pile of leaves. We figured we could bury her when things calmed down. When we came back, she was breathing! Just barely. My mother held her close for warmth, and my father and her father breathed in her mouth.

We were like animals in a jungle. The adults gave her drops of water in her mouth, sometimes even spitting into her mouth, and held her close to their bodies to give her warmth. They found pieces of food for her and gave her new life. They all gave her back her life.

She survived the war with her father—two out of seven in her family, and she had a wonderful life after the war.

Warm weather finally came again in the spring, and we moved to a different part of the forest because we were afraid shepherds from the villages would come to let their animals forage. We heard too many noises and went to a bunker about three or four miles away. When the leaves came out, we started living out in the open more, and we even built a little fire one time. We had no idea, none at all, what was going on outside—even if the war was over or not.

———

Once we were near a sort of orchard, and the trees were beginning to produce fruit, just the beginnings of the apples, very far from ripe. My brother went to get some, and we watched and waited for him. Suddenly, we saw men on horses!

There's a soldier on one horse and someone in civilian clothes with a rifle on another horse. A soldier with a rifle sat on a third horse. They had caught my brother stealing the apples and made him lead them to where he came from. When we saw them coming toward us with my brother, we knew it was the end. Again we said goodbye to each other and kissed each other. We didn't care anymore.

But it turned out to be the partisans! Soviet partisans! Liberation had come! A third miracle! I have never seen such tears, laughter, screaming, and hysterics. There was such a mix of emotions. Happiness that the worst of our hardships was over, we had survived, and deep, deep sadness about all those who were lost, who didn't get this far.

I looked up at my father and asked, "How did this happen? How did we survive?" Even as a child, I couldn't believe it. It made no sense. Why were we alive?

# CHAPTER SEVEN
# Darkness: Ryszard Witnesses

The third survivor, Ryszard Lubinski, was a childhood friend of Basia-Ruchel Potash in Trochenbrod. They were separated during the Holocaust: Basia-Ruchel's family hid in the forest, and Ryszard and his mother returned to Western Poland. Neither knew if the other was alive. Sixty years passed, and through a series of extraordinary—Betty says, miraculous—coincidences, they found each other again.

On one of my visits to Betty in Cleveland, she showed me a few photographs of Trochenbrod.

"Where did these come from?" I asked, amazed to see for the first time what the town my father grew up in had actually looked like. That's when I first learned the story of Betty's childhood friend, Ryszard, and his mother Janina, Trochenbrod's photographing

Catholic postmistress. At the first opportunity, I flew to Poland to meet Ryszard and record his story.

RYSZARD LUBINSKI, WITH THE AUTHOR (RIGHT), RADOM, POLAND, 2008.
*Photograph by Jeremy Goldscheider.*

JANINA LUBINSKI, 1928.
*Photographer unknown; photograph provided by Ryszard Lubinski.*

Not only was Ryszard the only non-Jew ever born in Trochenbrod, he was also the only non-Jew who went to school there until he was 12 years old. Although Catholic, Ryszard even today thinks of Trochenbrod as his home town. Ryszard and his mother remained in their home in Trochenbrod until winter 1942. Their home was the post office that was closed down by the Soviets in 1939. They were the only ones who lived in Trochenbrod before, during, and after the Holocaust. Ryszard remembers the town with deep affection. He also remembers Trochenbrod's last terrible days clearly.

Jews made Sofiyovka and developed it into a town that needed a post office. My mother took the job in Sofiyovka because she came from a town with a lot of Jews and was comfortable among them. I am alive today because of Sofiyovka Jews. Why? When the Russians took over in 1939, they wanted to send us to Siberia because they saw my mother as a Polish official and maybe a spy. But the Jews of Sofiyovka said no, and they begged the Russians to let us stay.

The Russians talked to the people in Sofiyovka, and then told my mother, "Everyone says that you are a good person and can be trusted, so we will not send you to Siberia. You can stay."

And Trochenbrod's Jews were good to her. For example, she couldn't even get water. Every time she would go out to get water—we had to walk a little bit to bring water from a well—some Sofiyovka man would see her and stop her and say, "No, no, I'll bring the water for you," and they would go to the well, fill up her bucket, and bring it back to our house. They respected her and wanted to help her.

The Sofiyovka children studied at the kheder every day. All my friends were there in the kheder. I had no one to play with, so I'd go and listen under the window of the kheder, especially in the summer when the windows were open, and I could hear what happened inside. They would learn in Hebrew by memorizing. Since I stood there listening, I also learned by memorizing. I couldn't read but would repeat the sounds over and over.

One time the teacher called on one of the boys to say several lines. He began reciting the lines, and at one point he made a mistake. That made the teacher very angry, and in the usual way, the teacher physically punished him and yelled, "Why do you say it wrong?"

Sometimes the teacher would hit the pupil's hand with a stick, and sometimes he would hold his mouth open and spit into it for saying a wrong answer. So the boy answered, "Ryszard told me."

But it wasn't true. I knew Yiddish as well as all my friends—I can still speak Yiddish today, especially after some vodka—and from listening at the kheder window I knew the Hebrew words better than some of my friends. Sometimes when I walked in the street, people said, "Look, this is the one who helps the Jewish boys in the kheder" because I really did whisper the answers sometimes to help my friends—but always the correct answer. I still remember Hebrew words.

I remember two oil presses in Sofiyovka. One was next to Eli

Potash's house, the other was owned by Szames. They were face-to-face on opposite sides of the street. They had very complicated machinery that would be in a museum today. Eli Potash had another house which was his workshop, next to the post office where we lived. The kheder was across the street from us and down a little bit. There was a synagogue a few houses farther down, with a very strange rabbi—he was very loud. When he prayed, you could hear him everywhere in Trochenbrod.

One time, after the Germans arrived, a strange person appeared in Sofiyovka: Dr. Klinger. He was about 50 years old when he came. To me, as a child he seemed very old. He had a lot of scars around his face and on his hands, and some of his fingers were missing. He arrived in Sofiyovka as a German, dressed in a stylish way, and seemed to be an important person. The Germans showed him great respect. We wondered where he came from and where he got his scars and lost his fingers.

He was often a guest in our house. He began to trust us as friends, and he told us he was a Jew. He confided that while studying somewhere in Germany at the time of Kristallnacht, the Germans attacked him with knives. He protected his face with his hands, and as a result he lost some fingers and has scars all over. The scars let him pretend he was a veteran of World War I, and his wounds brought him a lot of honor among the Germans.

Dr. Klinger convinced the Germans that he needed some of Trochenbrod's Jews for leather work and protected a lot of them for a while. But some of the Shutsmen were suspicious. They insisted he come with them for a drink one night and got him very drunk. When he was drunk and helpless, they undressed him and saw he was circumcised. They dragged him to the street and shot him. His body stayed there overnight until Jews came and took him away to bury him.

Before the Germans had the first aktion, they prepared the townspeople. A big-shot German came and gave a speech that no one will be hurt if they followed orders and did not behave wrongly. The Germans had been in charge of the town for a long time, and there had been murders, but no mass killing. One day, the special killing unit of German soldiers arrived in Sofiyovka with assistants of Ukrainian Shutsmen who surrounded the town. No one suspected that they would be killed. They thought, Oh, another one of the German big shots will give a speech and it will be over. So there was no big resistance.

During the first aktion, my mother hid 60 people in the attic of the post office. They survived until the second aktion.

There was a Polish man in the nearby village of Yosefin. He had fought in World War I. He was a man who knew how to use weapons, a strong man, a commanding person. He was working in his fields on the day of the first aktion and saw and heard what was happening. Something snapped in his head, and he became a completely different person, walking around in a daze, mumbling words no one could understand. The next day, he put on a coat and told people he was going to search for Free Poland. No one ever saw him again.

More people escaped into the forest from the second aktion because it was not so well organized as before. The Germans thought that with so many less people than the first aktion, they didn't have to be as careful. But now the Jews knew what was going to happen. They were better prepared, and more escaped. The beans in the fields behind the houses in Trochenbrod were on tall frames. When running from the Germans, people would sometimes run among the beans because that would hide them, and then they would run in the drainage canals.

I've thought about Trochenbrod often all these years. I still miss it. I remember eating gefilte fish there. Since then, I've tried it sometimes, but nothing came close to the way it tasted in Sofiyovka. Even when my mother made it, after we came here to Radom, it was not as good as it was when the mothers of my friends gave it to me in Sofiyovka. That was really in the Jewish style.

Whenever I walk in the street and smell cooking of a food like there was in Trochenbrod, I think "Oh, that smells like Sofiyovka," and pictures of Sofiyovka come to my mind. I remember latkes—ahh, latkes—and chulunt in the oven for the Sabbath. I can smell it now; I can almost taste it. When I think of Sofiyovka, I don't think of the mass murders there; I think of the life. Laughter, wonderful food, games, happiness, friends, weddings, holidays, warm families.

But I can never forget what it felt like as a child when everybody in Sofiyovka was murdered. When I went for water, I saw dead bodies everywhere. Looking down the street of Trochenbrod,

## *The* LOST TOWN

I saw only empty houses where the families of my friends lived. The doors and windows of the empty houses swung this way and that way in the wind, once in a while hitting the sill with a soft bang, and then with hinges squeaking they swung again. Where are my friends? Where are their families? What happened to my Trochenbrod?

# CHAPTER EIGHT
## The Story Continues

LIGHT
by Yisrael Beider

Don't despair my brother dear,
If in the west day's end seems near.
I beg hold fast these words of mine,
After this darkness a light will shine.

I also found this poem, originally in Hebrew, among those newspaper clippings my father had saved. Just like the poem "On the Water," his brother, Yisrael, wrote and probably published it around 1939 in *HaKochav* (*The Star*), a Hebrew language monthly published in Poland. *HaKochav* published many Hebrew poems by Yisrael Beider.

## *The* LOST TOWN

In the 70 years since the town vanished, what happened to the place where Trochenbrod stood? I've been back to the site of Trochenbrod and the villages around it many times. Each time, I sought out people, especially older people, who could tell me both about Trochenbrod and what had transpired at the site since it vanished. The story was fairly easy to piece together from their consistent accounts.

After Trochenbrod's Jews were murdered, the German Army used its land to supply food for its soldiers. A military man who knew how to run a large farm was brought in, and he established a forced labor system for people from the surrounding villages. They cultivated the land of Trochenbrod, now his farm. He made the villagers build him a house near where the last Trochenbrod synagogue had been, on the north end of town where today a black marble monument stands. For the house and for several other new farm buildings, he had them use materials left from destroyed Trochenbrod houses and buildings. The German Army farm had horses, goats, cows, and chickens, and the villagers cultivated potatoes, beans, corn, cabbage, and other local crops for German soldiers.

The Germans' farm did not survive more than one growing season. In the fall of 1943, fighters from a partisan detachment, the one Khaim Votchin was in, surrounded the Trochenbrod area and set fire to as many buildings as they could. The German farm manager escaped to German units near the city of Rovno and was never seen again.

Following the war, no one made use of Trochenbrod's land for about 10 years. The reasons why it was unused before the first Jews settled there 130 years earlier were the same reasons why it was unused this time. The quality of the soil was poor, the area was a marshy lowland, and it was a considerable distance from transportation routes in the region. In addition, under the Soviet Communists who ruled the area after the war, local markets were not allowed, and individual families did not have horses or tractors. Local people had no real reason to cultivate Trochenbrod's land and did not have the equipment to cultivate it if they wanted to.

In the mid-1950s, the Soviets decided they could not leave such a large parcel of what had once been farmland unused. They made modest improvements to prepare the land for farming, and in 1957, assigned the area that had been Trochenbrod and its satellite villages to a collective farm they named Nove Zhyttia—New Life. All villages in western Ukraine had been forced to operate as parts of collective farms by this time, and Nove Zhyttia was headquartered in Domashiv, one of the villages nearest to Trochenbrod. As Soviet rule continued, a generation was being born in Domashiv and other villages of the area that only knew communism and life under the Soviets. They had no idea that a town, a Jewish town, had not long ago bustled there with commerce.

In 1991, Ukraine became an independent country and collective farms ended. Today, you may find local people grazing their horses, and sometimes you'll see one or two fields sown in grass or clover for animals. But Trochenbrod's land today remains basically unused. It is an empty clearing in the forest, owned by the government that has no plans for it. Not many people in the surrounding villages have any idea what used to be there.

And yet Trochenbrod/Sofiyovka, sometimes has a mysterious passing presence for local people, almost like an unknown ghost that hovers in the air from time to time. Once I stood in a Trochenbrod field when my Ukrainian friend from Domashiv asked if I'd like to find a memento from the town at Leah's house. Leah's house? No one knows why the place is called Leah's house. We drove by tractor to what would have been the southern end of Trochenbrod and dug in the soil near a big fruit tree. In the ground, I found a piece of what must have been one of the plates with which Leah had set her table.

I once walked by a farmer's yard in the area and noticed a stack of paving stones piled close to the wall of his house. The paving stones reminded me of the ones I had seen in the photograph of the ribbon-cutting ceremony for the short segment of road that was paved in Trochenbrod. The farmer was in his yard, so I asked him where he got the stones.

"From Sofiyovka," he answered, and he jerked his head in the direction of where Trochenbrod used to be, as if to say, "In the next village, over there."

There is an acre of land not far from the black marble monument called the Shwartz field, once occupied by buildings of Trochenbrod's wealthy Shwartz family. When I asked about it to

TROCHENBROD PAVING STONE HELD BY EVA KURNYEVA, 2006.
*Photograph by the author.*

see what the local people knew of their history, I found some village young people had never given a thought to what the name might have meant. Others vaguely guessed someone named Shwartz once lived there. Old people sometimes went silent and looked as if old memories had been awakened.

———

On August 18, 2009, three Trochenbrod old-timers gathered in the Ukrainian village of Domashiv together with 70 descendants of Trochenbrod families. Two of the old-timers were Holocaust survivors who lived to tell the tale by hiding in the forest. The third had slipped away during the Russian occupation. People gathered from Brazil, Canada, Israel, Ukraine, and the United States. They made their way in a procession of 15 horse-drawn wagons through Domashiv farm fields and then through abandoned acreage to the site of Trochenbrod. They deliberately traveled using the same means of transportation the people of Trochenbrod had used.

Betty Gold (Basia-Ruchel Potash) was there. Another was Evgenia Shvardovskaya, who also survived by hiding in the forest with her family. Evgenia was frail, but her grandson, who headed the small Jewish community in Lutsk, came back to Trochenbrod with her and helped her. The one who slipped away before the Germans came was Shmulik Potash. With their first-person stories, these people brought Trochenbrod alive for the captivated descendants. They discovered a feeling of connection to this place, a sense of identity with this vast field somewhere in Ukraine that they had never seen before. They discovered within the group, relatives from other countries that they had never met and in some cases did not know existed. They felt a kinship with each other that left them singing and laughing together as family.

The languages of the visitors were English and Hebrew. The Ukrainian wagon drivers who brought their horses and wagons from neighboring villages, some Ukrainian friends and well-wishers from Domashiv and Lutsk, and dozens of their children watched respectfully from a short distance. Some had tears in their eyes and seemed to understand as they watched people make family connections, visit the graves of their ancestors, and recapture the history of the place. Now they wanted to know more about the history of the area, not just the history of Ukrainians. It was the first time most of them fully understood that many different types of people had lived in the area and made up its history.

Imagine, there was a Jewish town here! Now both the adults and children among them wanted to know more about their history—about that town and the people who lived in it.

# Trochenbrod Chronology

1791   Czarina Catherine the Great establishes Russia's Jewish Pale of Settlement, where most of Russia's Jews will be concentrated.

1804   Czar Alexander I decrees that Russia's Jews may live only in larger towns and cities of the Pale of Settlement. Jews who engage in agriculture on unused land are exempt. In the following years, the first Jewish families settle to farm in a marshy forest clearing.

*(Slavery is declared illegal in the northern states of the United States.)*

1813   Trochenbrod's first baby is born.

1820   A group of Jewish families from cities in the surrounding area joins the earlier Trochenbrod settlers.

1827   Czar Nicholas I decrees that Jewish teen-aged boys be taken into the Russian Army until age 45. A new surge of Jewish settlement at Trochenbrod follows.

*(The United States is just over 50 years old.)*

1828   Twenty-one Mennonite families establish the villages of Yosefin and Sofiyovka near Trochenbrod.

1837   Settlers establish Lozisht, also known as Ignatovka, near Trochenbrod as a sister Jewish agricultural "colony."

1865   Trochenbrod/Sofiyovka gains official town status; Lozisht/Ignatovka remains a colony.

*(America's Civil War ends.)*

1897   Trochenbrod and Lozisht together have a population of close to 1,600 Jews. Trochenbrod begins to modernize and diversify into a broad array of economic activities, including light industry. It has become the regional commercial center.

*(1901 Teddy Roosevelt becomes President of the United States.)*

1914   Trochenbrod is on the front between Austro-Hungarian and Russian troops in World War I and suffers terribly.

*(1918 World War I ends.)*

1921   Trochenbrod now falls within Eastern Poland.

1929   The Polish *Illustrated Directory of Volyn* describes Sofiyovka as a robust, regional commercial center.

*(The Great Depression begins in the United States.)*

1933   In this year and the next, many Trochenbroders who immigrated to the United States return to visit their relatives in Trochenbrod. One of them took the photograph on the cover of this book.

*(1934 Hitler emerges as a major political figure in Europe.)*

1939 Trochenbrod falls under Soviet rule as World War II begins.

1940 Following the German invasion of Western Poland, an influx of Jewish refugees swells the population of Trochenbrod and Lozisht from 5,000 to 6,000.

1941 June: Germany invades and the Soviets withdraw from Eastern Poland, leaving Trochenbrod in Nazi hands.

*(December: Pearl Harbor is attacked. America enters World War II.)*

1942 August: The first aktion. Most of the Jews of Trochenbrod and Lozisht are murdered.

September: The second aktion. Everyone remaining in Trochenbrod's ghetto is murdered.

December: The third aktion. The last few alive, about 20 leather workers, are shot.

*(1945 World War II ends.)*

1950 A Trochenbrod survivor living in the nearby city of Lutsk reports that she visited the site of Trochenbrod and found no remaining physical evidence of it.

# Sources

1. Morris Wolfson, "A Grandfather's Memories." Oral memoir of Morris Wolfson as told to his granddaughter, Geri Wolfson Fuhrmann, November, 1974.

2. Nahum Kohn and Howard Roiter, *A Voice from the Forest: Memoirs of a Jewish Partisan,* (New York: Holocaust Library, 1980).

3. *And I Still See Their Faces: Images of Polish Jews,* (Warsaw, Poland: American-Polish-Israeli Shalom Foundation, 1997).

4. Tuvia Drori, *Ani Ma'amin: Eidut V'Hagot (I Believe: Testimony and Meditations),* (Tel Aviv, Israel:Yair Publications, 1994).

5. Jacob Banai, *Anonymous Soldier,* (Tel Aviv, Israel: Friends Publishing, 1978).

6. Gad Rosenblatt, *Esh Achazah B'ya'ar (A Forest Ablaze),* (Kibbutz Lochamei Haghettaot, Israel: Hakibbutz Hameuchad Publishing House, Ltd., 1976).

7. "Findings of the [Soviet] Commission Documenting Fascist Atrocities," (Lutsk, Ukraine: State Archives of the Volyn Region, 1945).

8. Y. Vainer, T. Drori, G. Rosenblatt, and A. Shpielman, eds., *Hailan V'shoreshav (The Tree and Its Roots: The History of T.L., Sofiyovka-Ignatovka,* (Givatayim, Israel: Bet Tal, 1988).

9. Father Patrick Desbois, *The Holocaust by Bullets: A Priest's Journey to Uncover the Truth Behind the Murder of 1.5 Million Jews,* (New York: Palgrave Macmillan, 2008).

10. *Ilustrowany Przewodnik po Wolyniu (Illustrated Directory of Volyn),* (Warsaw, Poland 1929).

11. W. M. Gdanskiem, *Księga Adresowa Polski (Polish Address Directory), 1929,* (Warsaw, Poland: Towarzystwo Reklamy Międzynarodowe, 1929).

12. Helmut T. Huebert (text and maps) and William Schroeder (maps), *Mennonite Historical Atlas,* 2nd edition, (Winnipeg, Canada: Springfield Publishers, 1996).

13. David Shwartz, *My Townlet—Trachenbrod: A Chain of Memories,* (Tel Aviv, Israel: Elisha Press, 1954).

14. Shmuel Spektor, *Pinkas Hakehilot (Encyclopedia of Jewish Communities from their Founding until Just after the Holocaust and Second World War), Volume 5, Volyn and Polesia,* (Jerusalem, Israel: Yad Vashem, The Holocaust Remembrance Martyrs and Heroes Remembrance Authority, 1990).

15. Jeanne Glass Kokol, "Russia to New York." 2002.

16. Shmilike Drossner, "Shmilike Drossner's Trachenbrod." Oral history by Shmilike Drossner told to and transcribed by Samuel Sokolow, 1970s.

17. Gad Rosenblatt, "Sofievka (Trochenbrod)," (Jerusalem: Archives of Yad Vashem, The Holocaust Martyrs and Heroes Remembrance Authority, 1970s).

18. Eliezer Barkai (Burak), "Trochenbrod (Sofiyevka)," Yalkut Volyn (Anthology of Volyn) no. 1, (Tel Aviv: Volyn Archives in the Land of Israel, April, 1945).

19. Morton L. Kessler, MA Thesis: "Trochenbrod: The Life and Death of a Shtetl in the Ukraine," (Cleveland: Graduate School of John Carroll University, 1972).

Other sources that I drew upon for this book include:

- Dozens of photographs provided by families descended from Trochenbroders
- Videotapes of elderly individuals reminiscing about their lives in Trochenbrod that were given to me by their respective descendants
- Austro-Hungarian, German, Polish, Russian, Soviet, Ukrainian, and US military maps spanning the period 1706-2006
- Interviews I conducted with people born in Trochenbrod or living in nearby villages, recorded in Israel, Brazil, the United States, and Ukraine
- Interviews I conducted and recorded with a number of Ukrainians living in the Trochenbrod area who remembered Trochenbrod from their childhood or youth
- Conversations with Ukrainians who now live or used to live in villages near the site of Trochenbrod, who told me stories they heard from their parents
- My explorations of Trochenbrod's terrain by foot and tractor with my friend, Ivan Podziubanchuk, and his family from the nearby village of Domashiv, during my 12 visits to the area from 1997 to 2014

# Acknowledgments

I want to thank my wife, Leah, who encouraged me and gave me invaluable editorial advice (which I took) and has happily been my partner and best friend for well over 50 years.

And I want to thank our kids, Oren, Naftali, and Ronnit, for being such a great bunch of kids, and an inspiration, together with *their* kids, to put together this book.

Michele Orwin, of Bacon Press Books, has been a wonderful partner in the endeavor to bring *The Lost Town* to life. Thank you, Michele, for your guidance and support, and for the enormous effort you put into the publication of this book.

Special thanks to Lorraine Fico-White of Magnifico Manuscripts, to Alan Pranke of AMP 13, and to Lorie DeWorken of Mind the Margins for their editorial, artistic, and design contributions to the final manuscript and final appearance of this book.

My deepest gratitude to Merrill Leffler, of Dryad Press, for his invaluable editorial guidance, and also to Karen MacPherson and John Williamson for their editorial advice.

I will be eternally grateful to the many people on whom I leaned for the stories, memoirs, and other materials, and also help and advice, that enabled me to discover and write about Trochenbrod's unique story, including:

Michlean Amir, USA

Marvin Bendavid, USA

Doreen Berne, USA

Charles and Marilyn Bernhardt, USA

Miriam Antwarg Ciocler, Brazil

Mikhailo Demchuk, Ukraine

Tuvia Drori, Israel

Alexander Dunai, Ukraine

Geri Wolfson Fuhrmann, USA

Mary Lou Garbin, USA

Betty Gold (Basia-Ruchel Potash), USA

Betty Hellman (Peshia Gotman), USA

Helmut T. Huebert, Canada

Anatoliy Hrytsiuk, Ukraine

Anna, Eva, and Ivan Kurnyev, Ukraine

Andrea Liss, USA

Ida Gilden Liss, USA

Ryszard Lubinski, Poland

Panas Mudrak, Ukraine

Loiko Mykytivna, Ukraine Vladislav Nakonieczny, Ukraine

Sergiy Omelchuk, Ukraine

Ivan and Nina Podziubanchuk, Ukraine

Shmuel (Shmulik) Potash, Israel

Laura Praglin, USA

Yale J. Reisner, Poland and USA

Szoel Rojtenberg, Brazil

Meylakh Sheykhet, Ukraine

Vira Shuliak, Ukraine

Evgenia Shvardovskaya, Israel and Ukraine

Burt and Ellen Singerman, USA

Gary Sokolow, USA

Hana Tziporen, Israel

Chaim Votchin, Israel

Anne Weiner, USA

# About the Author

Avrom Bendavid-Val was working as an environmental consultant in Poland in 1997 when he decided to cross the Ukrainian border and visit the place his father came from, the town of Trochenbrod. Finding nothing there, he was determined to uncover the history and spirit of the vanished town. Avrom continues to this day to research, write, and make films about the town, and serve as the anchor for the American community of Trochenbrod descendants. Avrom Bendavid-Val lives in Washington, DC.

www.ingramcontent.com/pod-product-compliance
Lightning Source LLC
Chambersburg PA
CBHW020110020526
44112CB00033B/1156